PUZZLES AND THINKING GAMES

Written by: Penny Holland
                   Carole Kubota
Project Manager: Marcia Shank
Consulting Editors: Ann de la Sota
                   Dennis J. Graham

Table of Contents

Snapshot Surprises

Classify these tricky pictures. Careful—they can fool you!

 Seen close up, even the most ordinary object can appear to be something else.

In a photographic closeup, everything is exaggerated—"larger than life." The resulting image can be surprising!

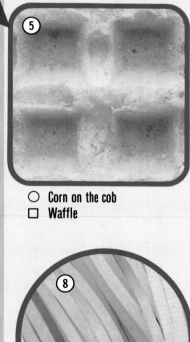

Answers

Look at the numbered photographs below. Can you tell what each is? For each photo, you are given two identification choices. Choose either ○ or □.

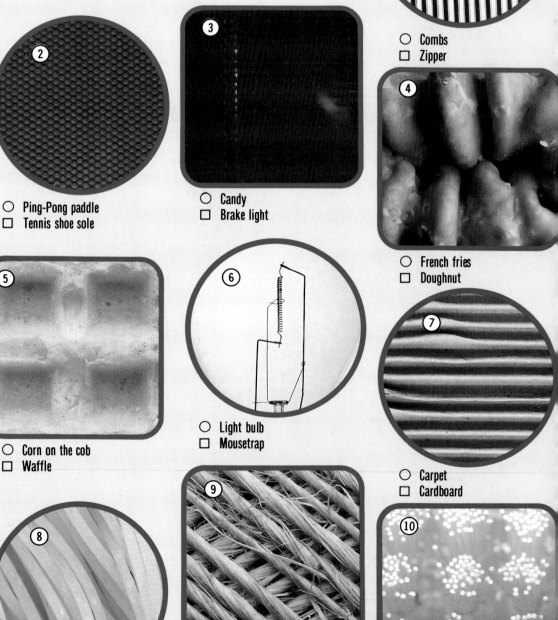

1

○ Combs
□ Zipper

2

○ Ping-Pong paddle
□ Tennis shoe sole

3

○ Candy
□ Brake light

4

○ French fries
□ Doughnut

5

○ Corn on the cob
□ Waffle

6

○ Light bulb
□ Mousetrap

7

○ Carpet
□ Cardboard

8

○ Spaghetti
□ Rubber bands

9

○ Twine
□ Broom

10

○ Powdered sugar
□ Toothbrush

Don't let the crazy quantities in these photographs fool you. Look carefully at each numbered picture, and figure out what it shows. Then select the answer from one of the three boxes marked ○ , △ , or □ .

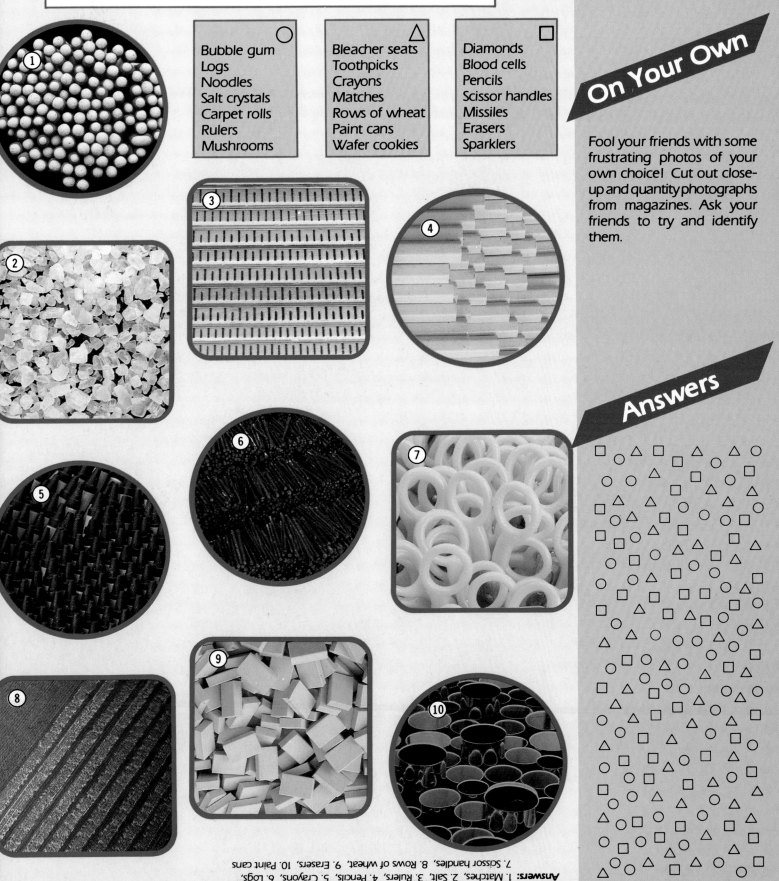

○
Bubble gum
Logs
Noodles
Salt crystals
Carpet rolls
Rulers
Mushrooms

△
Bleacher seats
Toothpicks
Crayons
Matches
Rows of wheat
Paint cans
Wafer cookies

□
Diamonds
Blood cells
Pencils
Scissor handles
Missiles
Erasers
Sparklers

On Your Own

Fool your friends with some frustrating photos of your own choice! Cut out close-up and quantity photographs from magazines. Ask your friends to try and identify them.

Answers

Answers: 1. Matches, 2. Salt, 3. Rulers, 4. Pencils, 5. Crayons, 6. Logs, 7. Scissor handles, 8. Rows of wheat, 9. Erasers, 10. Paint cans

Animal Codes

Try decoding these animals' symbols. It's easy as I, Г, ∧I

 he animals at Seaside Zoo's Special Care Clinic have codes on their hips. Caretakers use these codes to keep track of which animal goes where. Can you help them?

Look at the code on each animal. Then look at the special arrangement of numbers and shapes in the Code Key at the top of the picture to figure out each animal's number. Find that number on a caretaker's clipboard, and decide if the animal needs:

○ Further care
△ To be trained
□ To be returned to its natural habitat

Answers

CODE KEY

```
        3
   2        4
9     — = 0     5
      I = 1
   8        6
        7
```

Need further care
506 733
369 370

To be trained
648 320
915 145

Return to natural habitat
482
281

Seaside Zoo

The veterinarian at the zoo is going to examine the animals today. He has their medical records, but how will he know which animal is which? By their codes, of course! Look at each numbered medical record below. Then choose the code that the vet must look for to be sure he has the correct animal. Use the Code Key at the bottom of the page to help you figure out the correct codes.

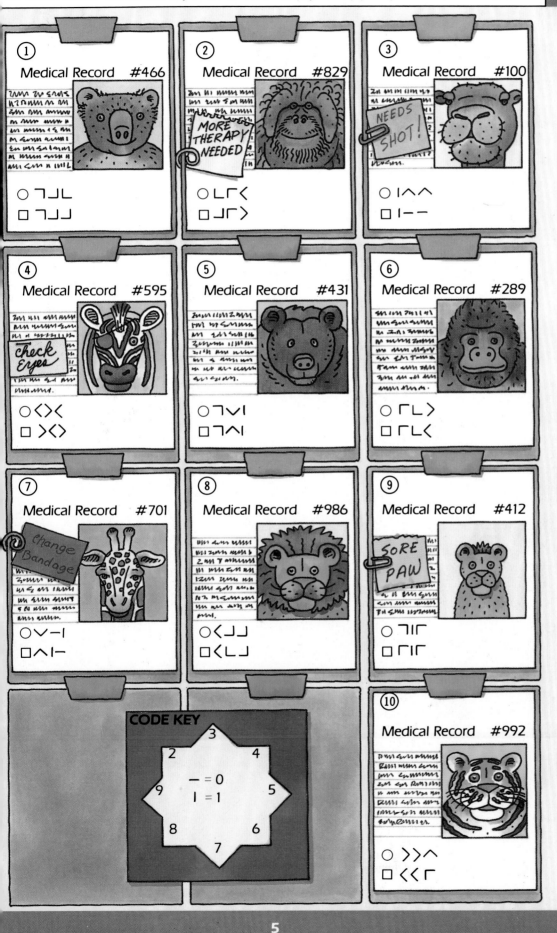

On Your Own

The code shown on these pages really is used to identify animals at zoos and marine parks. It is clipped or shaved in the animal's fur. This code is called the Farrel Numbering System. Write your telephone number and birthdate using the Farrel Numbering System. Copy the Code Key and give it and your "coded" numbers to a friend to decode.

Answers

5

Picture These Riddles

Solve these picture riddles and decide for yourself whether or not a picture is worth a thousand words!

 icture riddles are fun to figure out. Just put on your thinking cap and get started!

Look at each picture riddle and try to figure out what well-known expression or word it depicts. Then look for that expression in one of the three boxes marked ○, △, or □ . When you find it, select the symbol for that box as your answer.

Answers

○
A Point in Time
All Around the World
Pass the Sugar, Please
Prairie Dog Town
Square Dance Contest

△
All in All
Paradise
Little House on the Prairie
Time is Running Out
Dance to the Music

□
Pretty Please with Sugar on Top
Time on Your Hands
Sitting on Top of the World
All or Nothing
Alphabet Blocks

Look at each picture riddle below and try to figure out what well-known expression or word it depicts. Then look for that expression in one of the three boxes marked ○, △, or □. When you find it, select the symbol for that box as your answer.

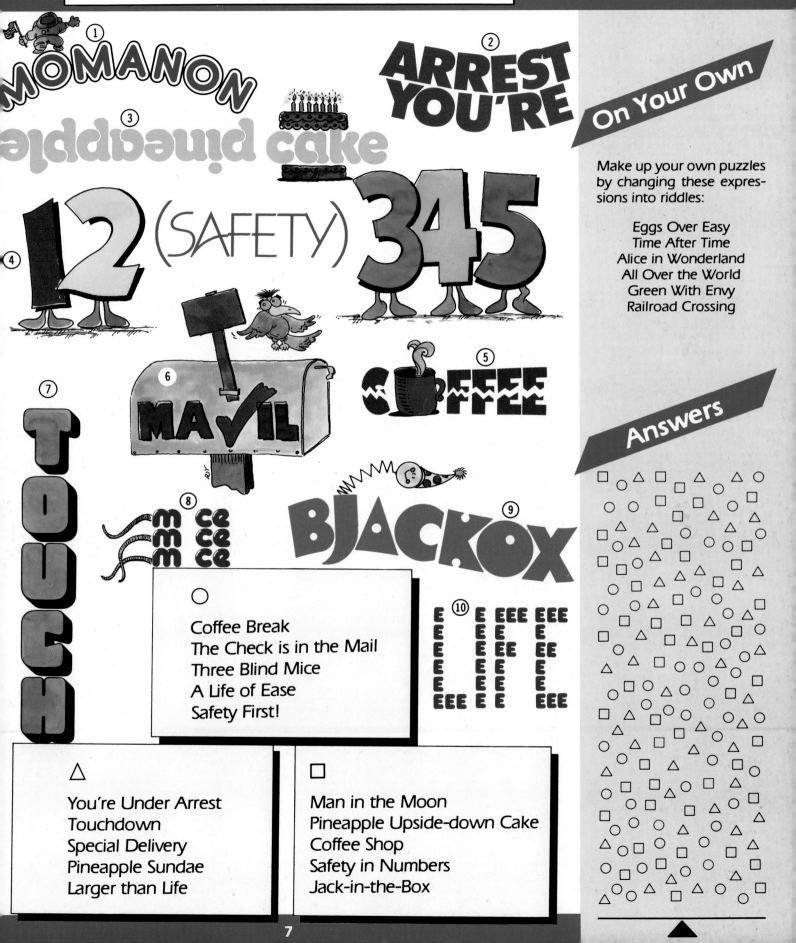

Make up your own puzzles by changing these expressions into riddles:

Eggs Over Easy
Time After Time
Alice in Wonderland
All Over the World
Green With Envy
Railroad Crossing

Answers

1. MOMANON
2. ARREST YOU'RE
3. əlddɒəniq cake
4. 12 (SAFETY) 345
5. C☕FFEE FFEE
6. MAVIL ✓
7. TOUCH
8. MMM CE CE CE
9. BJACKOX
10. EEE / EEE / EEE LIFE EEE

○
Coffee Break
The Check is in the Mail
Three Blind Mice
A Life of Ease
Safety First!

△
You're Under Arrest
Touchdown
Special Delivery
Pineapple Sundae
Larger than Life

□
Man in the Moon
Pineapple Upside-down Cake
Coffee Shop
Safety in Numbers
Jack-in-the-Box

Who's on First?

Join the Gorks, Snorks, Orks, Zonks, and Bloops for an intergalactic competition!

It's the highlight of the intergalactic sports year—the Worlds Series Spaceball Games! The action is about to begin, but to understand the game, you need to tell the teams apart.

Examine the fans in the picture to the right. Can you figure out in what two ways all Gorks are alike? All Snorks? All Orks?

Look at the numbered pictures below. Decide if each player is:

○ A Gork   △ A Snork   □ An Ork

Answers

The stadium at the Worlds Series Spaceball Games is filled with creatures from all over the Galaxy. Sitting in the bleachers below are the Zonks and the Bloops. Look at each group carefully. Can you figure out in which three ways all Zonks are alike and in which three ways all Bloops are alike?

Look at the refreshment stand below. Decide which of the numbered creatures are Zonks and which are Bloops.

○ This is a Zonk.   □ This is a Bloop.

On Your Own

On these two pages you have met Gorks, Snorks, Orks, Zonks, and Bloops. As you have seen, members of each group share common characteristics, but they can also look very different from each other. Draw a Gork, a Snork, an Ork, a Zonk, and a Bloop. Make them as fantastic as you wish, but be sure that each has the characteristics that all members of its group have.

Answers

Illusion Delusions

Is seeing believing? Sharpen your eyesight with these deceptive images.

n optical illusion is an image that misleads or deceives the eye. Each of the figures on this page is an optical illusion. Can you figure out what is real and what is not?

Look at each numbered illusion carefully, then answer the questions.

Answers

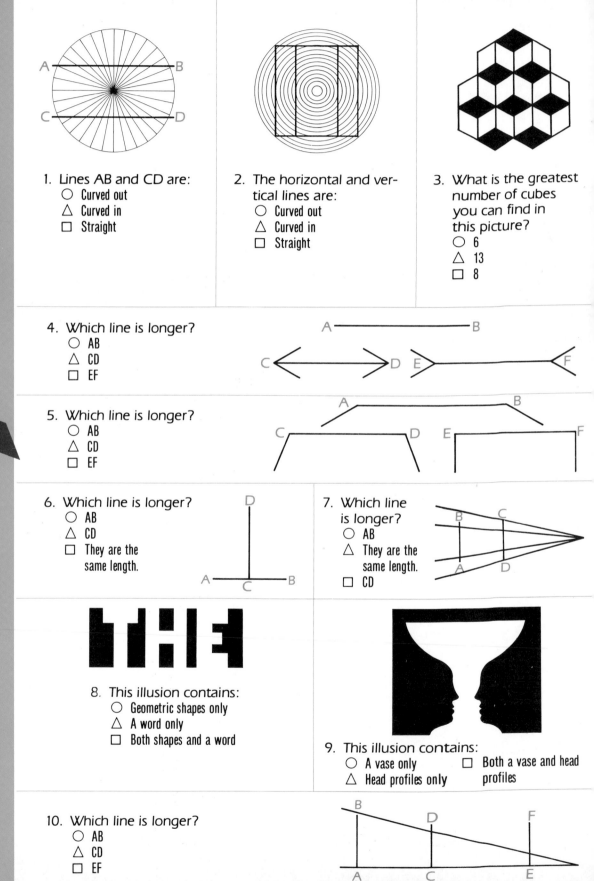

1. Lines AB and CD are:
   - ○ Curved out
   - △ Curved in
   - □ Straight

2. The horizontal and vertical lines are:
   - ○ Curved out
   - △ Curved in
   - □ Straight

3. What is the greatest number of cubes you can find in this picture?
   - ○ 6
   - △ 13
   - □ 8

4. Which line is longer?
   - ○ AB
   - △ CD
   - □ EF

5. Which line is longer?
   - ○ AB
   - △ CD
   - □ EF

6. Which line is longer?
   - ○ AB
   - △ CD
   - □ They are the same length.

7. Which line is longer?
   - ○ AB
   - △ They are the same length.
   - □ CD

8. This illusion contains:
   - ○ Geometric shapes only
   - △ A word only
   - □ Both shapes and a word

9. This illusion contains:
   - ○ A vase only
   - △ Head profiles only
   - □ Both a vase and head profiles

10. Which line is longer?
    - ○ AB
    - △ CD
    - □ EF

True or false? Look at each illustration, read the statement, and decide for yourself. Be careful . . . there may be more here than meets the eye!

○ True   □ False

1. Line AB is longer than Line CD.

2. Circle B is smaller than Circle A.

3. The gray areas of both squares are exactly the same shade.

4. Lines AB and CD are curved.

5. Lines AB and CD are the same length.

6. If Line A were extended it would meet Line B.

7. Line CD is longer than Line AB.

8. Lines AB and CD are the same length.

9. The height of the hat is greater than the width of the brim.

10. Figure C is taller than Figure A.

On Your Own

Draw your own optical illusion (or copy some of the ones on these pages) and try them on your friends.

Answers

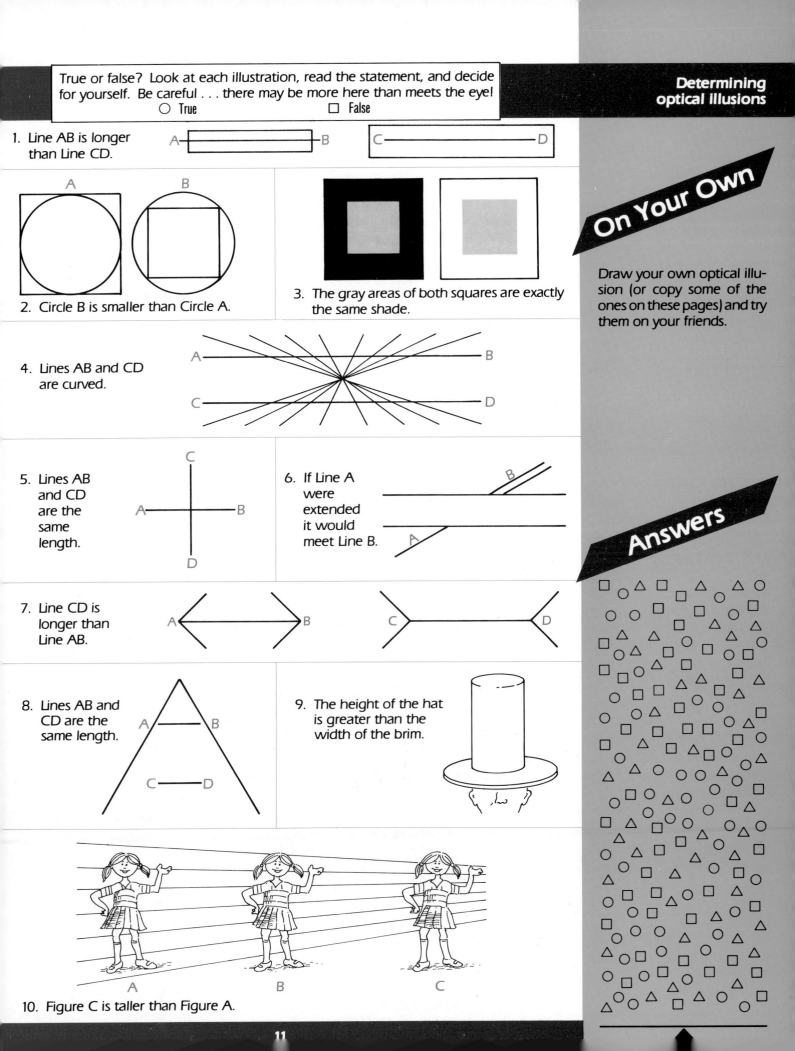

Stack Ups!

Stack up these puzzling pictures, but be sure that you assemble them in the correct order!

ook at the pictures on this page. A fussy chef has laid out his ingredients, left to right, in the order he wants them stacked from bottom to top. His cooks have prepared the snacks. They used all the proper ingredients, but they didn't always stack them correctly.

In each row match the three pictures on the left with the picture on the right that shows the snack stacked in its correct order. Choose ○, △, or □.

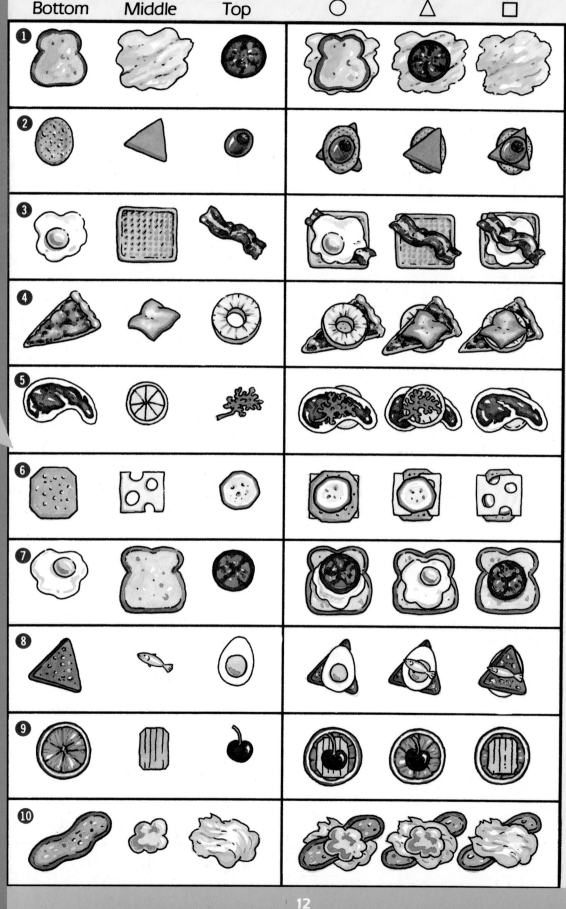

Look at the three shapes on the left side of this page. Then decide which picture on the right shows the correct order of these stack ups. Don't be fooled by the color change! Choose ○ , △ , or □ .

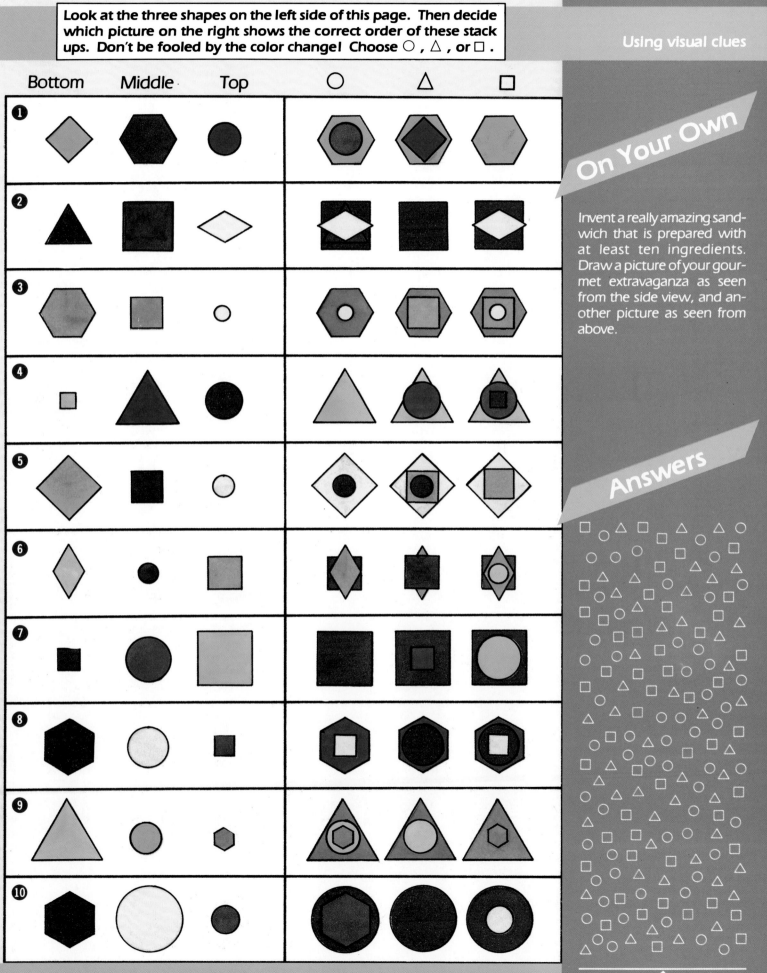

Invent a really amazing sandwich that is prepared with at least ten ingredients. Draw a picture of your gourmet extravaganza as seen from the side view, and another picture as seen from above.

Answers

Meet the Martians

Decide "who's who" and "who's going where" as you meet the Martians . . . and their friends!

 Alpha and Beta, a Martian couple, are very proud of their large family. They had a chart made that shows the relationships of their descendants.

Look at the arrangement of the pictures and then answer the questions on the top part of this page.

Hints:
- Picture frames connected by a ribbon indicate a married couple.
- A vertical line connects parents and their children.
- Male Martians are shown in square-shaped frames. Female Martians are shown in oval-shaped frames.

1. Who is Jotta's grandmother?
   ○ Hooga   △ Beta   □ Cheta
2. Who is Jotta's mother?
   ○ Cheta   △ Eta   □ Hooga
3. Who is Kappa's cousin?
   ○ Iota   △ Jotta   □ Delta
4. How many grandchildren does Alpha have?
   ○ four   △ three   □ two
5. Who is Cheta's father-in-law?
   ○ Alpha   △ Futa   □ Beta
6. How many nephews does Delta have?
   ○ two   △ one   □ three
7. How many nieces does Eta have?
   ○ two   △ three   □ one
8. Who is Iota's grandfather?
   ○ Gamma   △ Delta   □ Alpha
9. How many brothers does Hooga have?
   ○ three   △ four   □ one
10. How many brothers does Delta have?
    ○ three   △ two   □ one

Answers

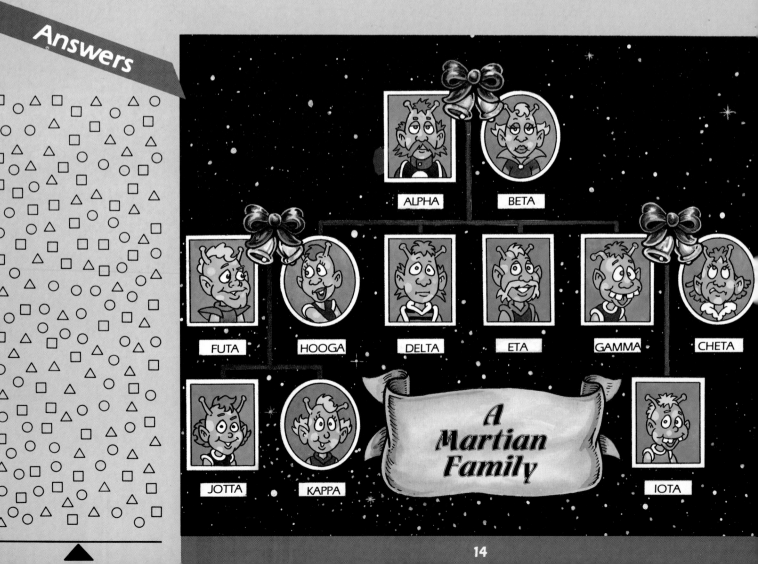

ALPHA   BETA

FUTA   HOOGA   DELTA   ETA   GAMMA   CHETA

JOTTA   KAPPA   IOTA

A Martian Family

It's Open House at the Annual Interplanetary Convention, and creatures from all over the galaxy are visiting each other's spaceships. The picture below shows the Martian, Plutonian, and Saturnian ships. As you can see from the maze of footprints, the Open House is well under way. Look at each numbered set of footprints. Then decide if it leads to the steps of:

○ The Martian spaceship
△ The Plutonian spaceship
□ The Saturnian spaceship

On Your Own

Create your own family tree. Start with one set of your grandparents, or even your great-grandparents, and work your way down to YOU! Use the chart on the left-hand page as a guide.

Answers

Mathmagics

Crank up Professor Tinker's FUNction machines for some mathematical fun!

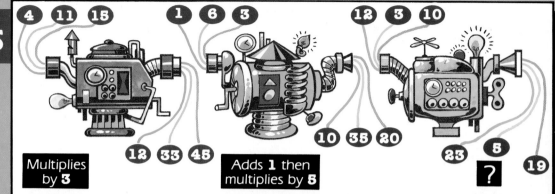

Multiplies by **3**

Adds **1** then multiplies by **5**

?

 oor absent-minded Professor Tinker! By accident, he used some of his Tinker's Amazing Disappearing Ink when he filled out parts of the chart to the right. Now some of his entries have completely vanished!

Help the professor complete his chart. Choose the correct answer on the right to complete each missing part of the chart.

Answers

Professor Tinker's Chart

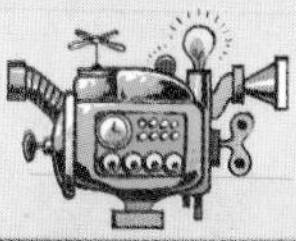

		○	△	□
		Subtracts 1 then doubles	Doubles then subtracts 1	Adds 9
① What does [machine] do?				
② 18 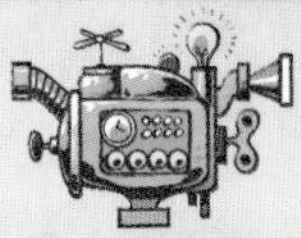	?	26	35	33
③ 15 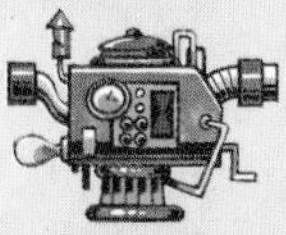	?	45	30	80
④ 11 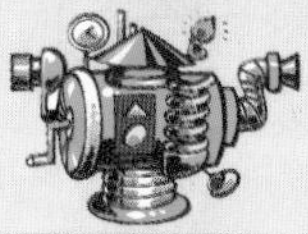	?	55	56	60
⑤ 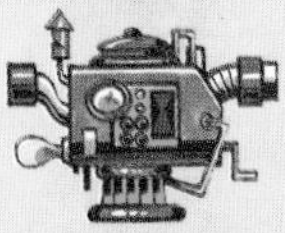 ?	120	40	12	30
⑥ 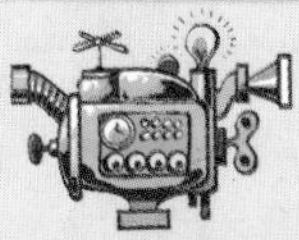 ?	99	50	33	19
⑦ 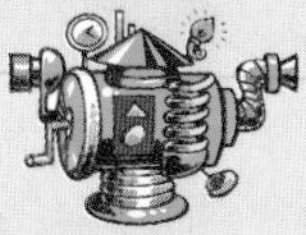 ?	55	27	11	10
⑧ 53 ?	105	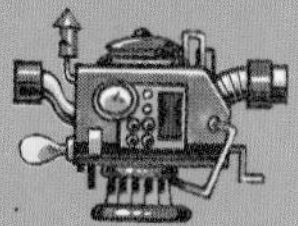	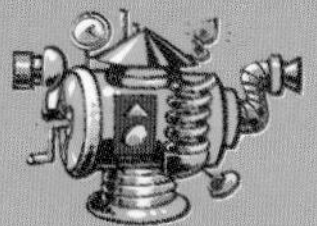	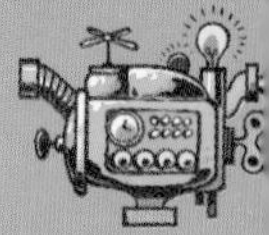
⑨ 48 ?	144	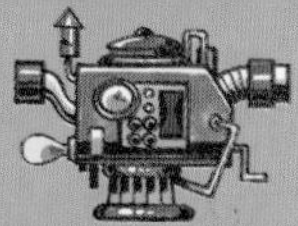	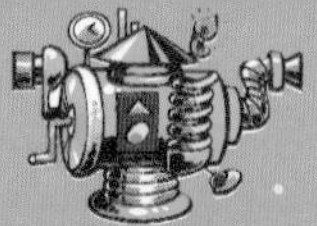	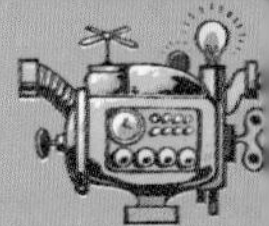
⑩ 85 ?	425	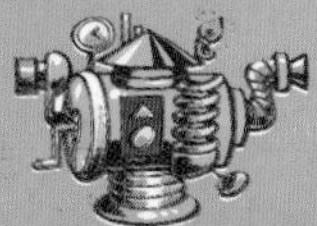	None of the machines	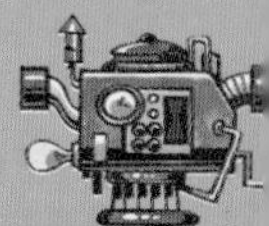

16

Clever Professor Tinker discovered that he could connect one function machine to another so that the output from one machine becomes the input for the next machine! Look at the professor's contraptions below and try to figure out how they work. Then select the correct answers to complete Tinker's chart.

4 11 15   **1 6 3**   **12 3 10**

12 33 45   **10 35 20**   **23 5 19**

Multiplies by **3**   Adds **1** then multiplies by **5**   Doubles then subtracts **1**

Deducing mathematical rules

On Your Own

Draw two or three function machines of your own. Tell what operation each one performs (Examples: "multiplies by 2," "adds 10," "doubles, then adds 4," etc.). Make up charts like those of Professor Tinker and give them to your friends to complete. (Be sure you know the correct answers first!)

Answers

		○	△	□
① 11 ➡ ?		166	165	170
② 10 ➡ ?		108	109	99
③ 37 ➡ ?		222	221	220
④ 37 ➡ ?		222	221	219
⑤ ? ➡ 45		3	2	5
⑥ ? ➡ 155		10	11	9
⑦ ? ➡ 150		14	15	12
⑧ ? ➡ 455		40	30	31
⑨ 12 ➡ ?		369	359	349
⑩ 12 ➡ ?		350	369	365

Transatlantic Translations

Are you sure you speak English? Test your "English" IQ and find out!

 he British and Americans share a common language, English, but we don't always call things by the same name. The picture to the right shows a scene filled with common items. You know what each is called in the United States. But do you know what they would be called in England?

Look at each numbered item in the picture. Then, from the list on this page, choose its correct "English" name.

1.	○ roundabout	□ lorry
2.	○ bonnet	□ jumper
3.	○ boot	□ kiosk
4.	○ rasher	□ mackintosh
5.	○ torch	□ tube
6.	○ plaster	□ cow gum
7.	○ pillar box	□ public convenience
8.	○ trolley	□ pushchair
9.	○ queue	□ petrol
10.	○ football	□ basketball

On Your Own

Watch a television program or movie that was filmed in England. Can you understand what is said? How many words or phrases are different from those you might say?

Now have a go at these tricky translations!

Read the cartoon story below. Then choose the correct definition for each underlined word in the story. Use the answer choices at the bottom of the page.

Oh, gosh! My jumper is gone! I must have left it at the big dipper! My mum will go bonkers when she hears about this! She just bought it for me a fortnight ago!

Relax, Ellen. Why don't you go check with the constable? I'll just nip over to the refreshment stand and get us a fizzy drink and some crisps.

But it's getting awfully late. I promised my mum I'd be back at the flat by 3 o'clock to babysit. And I have to pick up some nappies at the chemist before that.

We've got ages! It'll only take us 20 minutes to get home on the tube.

Oh, all right. You go queue up for the food and I'll meet you back here straightaway.

Answers

1. jumper	○ jump rope	☐ sweater
2. big dipper	○ roller coaster	☐ ice cream shop
3. fortnight	○ two days	☐ two weeks
4. constable	○ carnival owner	☐ police officer
5. fizzy drink and crisps	○ soda and potato chips	☐ milk shake and french fries
6. flat	○ shopping mall	☐ apartment
7. nappies	○ napkins	☐ diapers
8. chemist	○ hobby shop	☐ drug store
9. tube	○ subway	☐ bus
10. queue up	○ line up	☐ place an order

This 'n' That

 ERE is to THERE as THIS is to THAT. BARK is to DOG as MEOW is to CAT. HAT is to HEAD as LID is to PAN. Now solve these puzzles . . . if you can!

Look at the series of pictures on the left. Then choose the picture on the right that best completes each analogy.

Answers

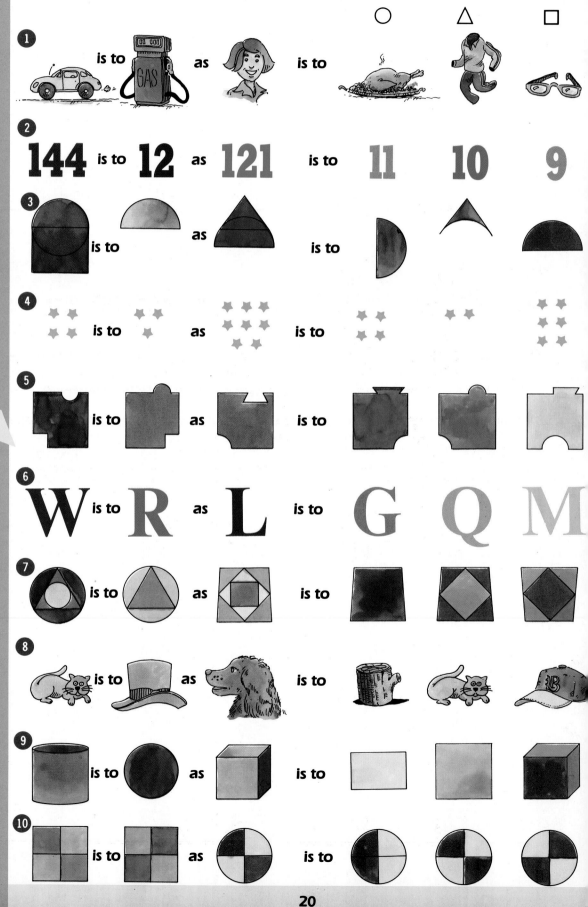

20

Here are more "this 'n' that" puzzles for you to solve!

On Your Own

Here's an analogy game that you can play. Pick two things that go together in some way, such as HAND and GLOVE. Now see how many ways you can finish this:

    Hand is to glove as
        (for example)
    foot is to sock.

Play this game with a friend. How many analogies can you come up with?

Answers

Reflecto's Magic

Figure out the magic behind Reflecto the Great's amazing illusions!

 eflecto the Great is about to say some magic words. Hocus Flippus! Presto Spin-o! Switcho Change-o! The pictures to the right show what happens when he says these mysterious words.

Examine the numbered picture pairs. Decide which magic words Reflecto said to change each picture on the left into the picture on its right.

Answers

○ **HOCUS FLIPPUS** flips my rabbit upside down . . .
like this!

△ **SWITCHO CHANGE-O** flips my rabbit from left to right . . .
like this!

□ **PRESTO SPIN-O** flips my rabbit upside down THEN flips it left to right . . .
like this!

1. MAY → YAM
2.
3.
4. 5 → ƨ
5.
6. 3/8 → 8/3
7.
8. COOK → COOK
9.
10.

In this mirror, what you see may not reflect reality at all! Look at the ten details at the bottom of this page. Then find the same details in the larger picture above. Compare each detail with its reflection in the mirror. Decide if the mirror reflection is:

○ A different shape △ Larger □ Smaller

On Your Own

Try making some of your own Hocus Flippus, Switcho Change-o, and Presto Spin-o puzzles. Give them to a friend and see if he or she can figure out which magic words were said!

Answers

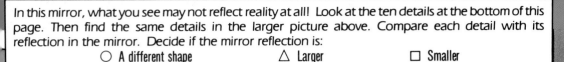

Do Opposites Attract You?

Look carefully! The answers to these puzzles may not be as plain as black and white.

o you know what a negative image is? The negative of a photograph is a piece of film in which the light and dark parts are in opposite positions from the original photo.

Each of the numbered pictures on this page has a negative—or opposite—image. For each drawing on the left, find its exact opposite among the drawings to the right.

Answers

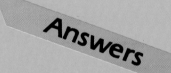

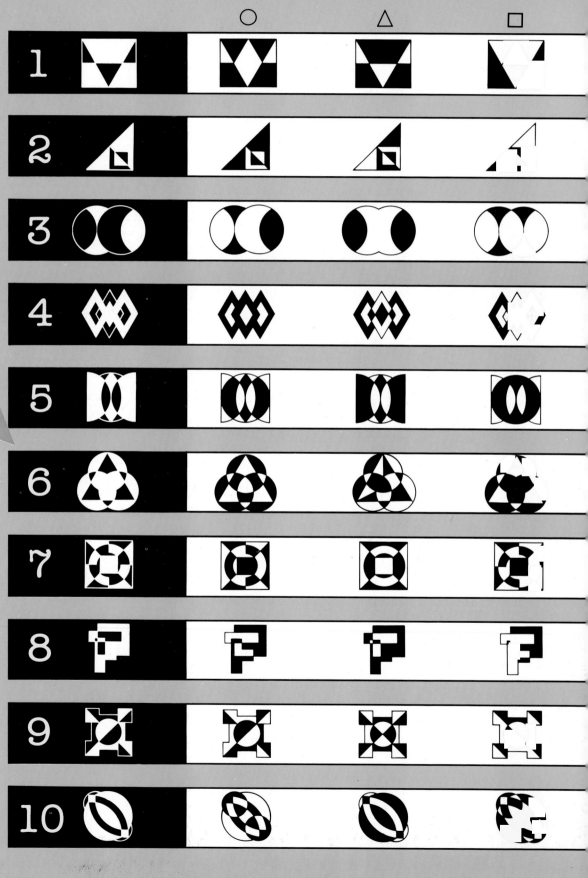

The figure to the right is called a color wheel. It shows the three primary colors (red, yellow, and blue) and the three secondary colors (orange, purple, and green). Colors that appear opposite each other on the color wheel are called opposite colors. As you can see, red and green are opposite colors. So are blue and orange, and yellow and purple.

Look at each numbered picture below. Then find the picture on the right that is the color opposite. Use the color wheel to help you.

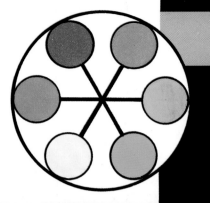

On Your Own

Using the color wheel on this page, create some opposite color designs of your own. Challenge your friends to find the designs that are exact color opposites of your originals.

Answers

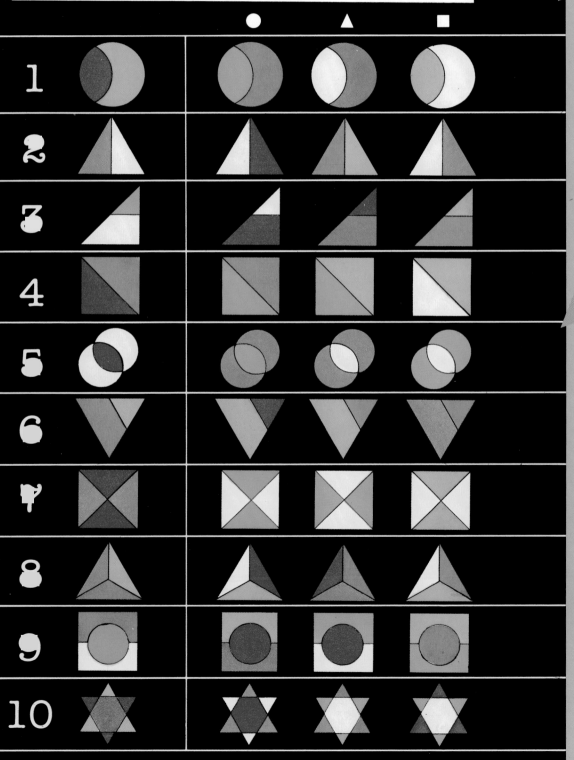

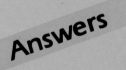

Jigsaw Jamboree

Pick up the pieces of these puzzles . . . then puzzle over where they belong!

 omeone in the jigsaw puzzle factory mixed extra pieces in with the puzzles. Can you find which pieces belong to the puzzle on this page, and which ones do not belong?

Look at each numbered puzzle piece, then decide if it:

○ Belongs to the puzzle
□ Does not belong to the puzzle

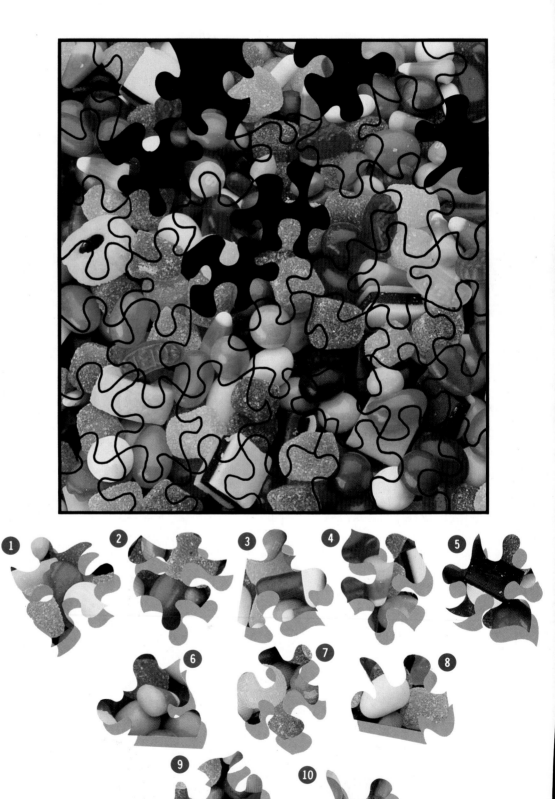

Both of these puzzles are almost completed, but each is missing some pieces. Examine each of the numbered puzzle pieces shown below and decide if it:

○ Belongs to Puzzle A   □ Belongs to Puzzle B

Puzzle A   Puzzle B

On Your Own

Cut your own jigsaw puzzle out of a poster, magazine picture, or a picture you draw yourself. For a sturdier puzzle, paste the picture on a piece of cardboard before you cut.

Answers

Sinkers and Stickers

Determine the fate of a cork, bolt, tennis ball, key, and a diamond ring! Which will sink and which will stick?

 You would probably guess that a rock thrown into water would sink. But could you be that certain about other objects?

Some of the objects on this page always sink when placed in water. Some always float. Others may sink or float! Which will do what? Examine each numbered object. Then decide if it:

○ Will always float
△ Will always sink
□ May sink or float

Answers

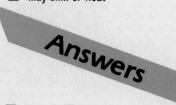

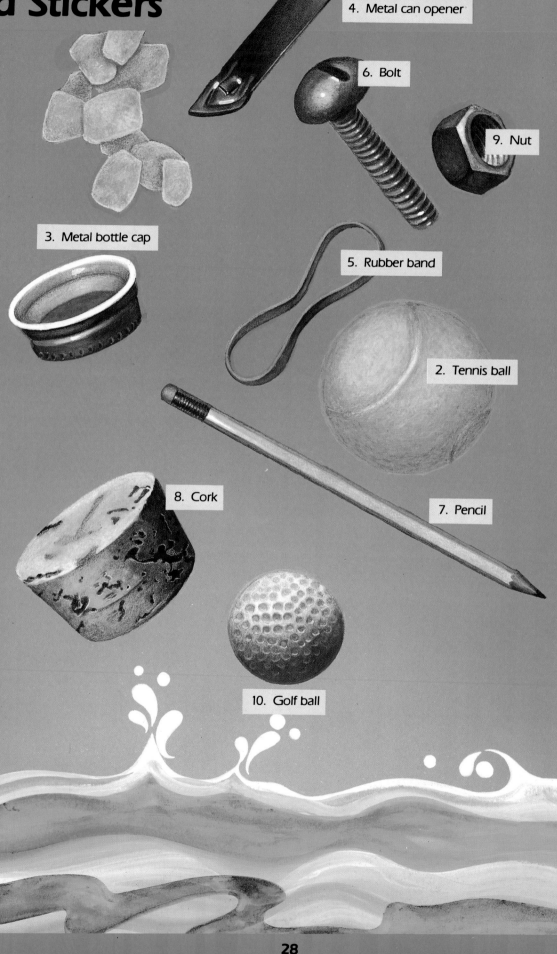

1. Cereal

4. Metal can opener

6. Bolt

9. Nut

3. Metal bottle cap

5. Rubber band

2. Tennis ball

8. Cork

7. Pencil

10. Golf ball

Only some of these objects will be attracted by the magnet. Your job is to guess which will and which won't!

Look at each numbered object below. Then decide if it would be:

○ Attracted by magnet
□ Not attracted by magnet

1. Stainless steel knife blade

2. Aluminum foil

5. Steel nail file

4. Metal hanger

3. Brass key

6. Nickel

10. Gold ring

7. Compass

9. Lead pencil

8. Metal paper clip

On Your Own

Try some "sink or stick" experiments of your own. Drop some objects into a bowl of water and see which sink and which float. (You might want to try some of the objects shown on the opposite page.) Get a magnet and discover what things it will attract . . . and what it won't.

Answers

It's All in How You Look at It

Go behind the scenes at a television studio and direct this rock group to stardom!

hree cameras are filming the scene to the right. It's the director's job to decide which pictures to use. It's not easy, because each camera films from a different angle and therefore shows something different.

Look at each numbered television screen and decide which camera is filming the picture. Choose camera ○, △, or □.

Answers

Match each picture with its correct silhouette.

○   △   □

On Your Own

Watch a television program and see if you can figure out how many different cameras are being used, and what their positions are. Can you tell when the program cuts from one camera to another?

Answers

INVENTIONS AND DISCOVERIES

Written by: Tina Harris
Deborah Nourse Lattimore
Erica Silverman
Anne F. Wittels
Project Manager: Ann de la Sota
Consulting Editors: Emilie Ferry
Dennis J. Graham
Pat Sarka
Marcia Shank
Lucy Vezzuto, Ph.D.

Table of Contents

Spinoffs from Space

Bring space technology down to Earth!

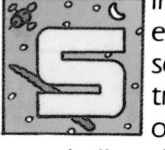ince the 1950's, enormous research on space travel has taken off! Lightweight metal alloys for space shuttles, new fibers for space suits, and new methods for relaying information over long distances are just a few of the things that have been developed.

Is all this research just for the benefit of astronauts? Not at all. Much of the technology generated by the space program is being adopted for use here on Earth!

Here is a list of ten inventions we use on Earth. Can you tell which things were originally invented for use in space, and which were originally invented for use on Earth?

○ Originally designed for space
□ Originally designed for Earth

1. Digital watch readout
2. Calculator
3. Solar-powered motor
4. Joystick control
5. Velcro fasteners
6. Weather satellite
7. Optacon reader
8. Metallic balloon fabric
9. Microwave oven
10. Plastic containers

On Your Own

Joysticks were originally designed for moon travelers. But we also use them on Earth to control vehicles, computers, and games. Can you think of three new uses for joysticks? Choose the idea you like best and draw a design for it.

Answers

Many intriguing inventions have been developed to fill specialized needs. Here is a sample.

Can't keep your shoelaces tied? Try Velcro! It wasn't originally designed for space, but it's often been used to hold space things in place.

Need to do some math problems quickly? So did space scientists; so they developed the calculator.

Want to harness energy from the sun? Nothing new about that! A French engineer made a solar-powered printing press in the 19th century. Today, solar power provides energy to operate many everyday items—from toy cars to television sets!

Do you know a handicapped driver? A joystick allows a driver to accelerate, brake, and steer a vehicle with just one hand. It was developed for astronauts driving the Lunar Rover on the Moon's surface.

Want to know if a storm is coming? Weather satellites, developed through space research, gather information to predict the weather.

Looking for a pretty gift? How about balloons made of metallic material? They last longer than flowers! Their light, strong, shiny fabric was originally designed for the space program.

Want something that can be molded in almost any shape? Plastic wasn't designed for space travel, but astronauts, like the rest of us, make good use of it.

Do you know the time, to the microsecond? A digital watch will tell you. Digital readouts were invented for the space program.

Want to heat food quickly, without a flame? Use a microwave oven. Scientists were experimenting with microwaves early in the space program.

Do you know there is a way for blind people to read without using Braille? Space optical technology developed the Optacon, a tiny camera that instantly transforms letters on a page to raised images on a board that a blind person can feel.

The Mad Hatter

Use your head to figure out what these wacky inventions were supposed to do.

eople have come up with some weird and wonderful inventions. Over the years, creative inventors have tried to provide what they thought people needed or wanted, often with funny results.

Here are ten inventions that are worn on the head. Some of them look as though they were designed by a mad hatter! Can you tell what each of these headgear items is?

1. ○ Anti-snoring device
   △ Anti-wrinkle device
   □ Football chin protector

2. ○ Cure for baldness
   △ Self-tipping hat
   □ Hat with cooling device

3. ○ Battle headgear
   △ Head protector for shipwrecks
   □ Gas mask

4. ○ Head-measuring device
   △ Hat with built-in compass
   □ Hat with built-in clock

5. ○ Rain hat
   △ Hang-glider hat
   □ Sunshade hat

6. ○ Toy hat
   △ Radio hat
   □ Fly-swatter hat

7. ○ Cure for dandruff
   △ Hair-cutting machine
   □ Permanent wave machine

8. ○ Headache-preventing hat
   △ Shoulder straightener
   □ Picnic-basket hat

9. ○ Rain or sun umbrella hat
   △ Acrobat's safety device
   □ Fire-escape parachute

10. ○ Easy-drink helmet
    △ Solar-powered fan helmet
    □ Spy telescope helmet

Did you ever go to a crazy hat party? Any of these would surely have won a prize for you!

Sunshade Hat
For the gentleman of 1890 who wanted to keep cool, Mr. Bartine invented a sunshade that fit over a bowler hat.

Apparatus to Prevent Snoring
Sleepers in 1871 could wear a leather device designed to hold the mouth closed. It probably prevented both snoring and talking in one's sleep!

Fire-Escape Parachute
In 1879 Oppenheimer designed a hat-parachute to ensure safe landings when people had to jump out of burning buildings.

Hair-cutting Machine
In 1951 people who wanted an even haircut could use John Boax's machine that sucked hair up and burned the ends to the proper length.

Toy Hat
A child of 1966 who wore this hat could make the streamer twirl by moving his or her head in a circle.

Headache-preventing Hat
If the ladies of 1912 suffered headaches from their tight hats, help was available from a frame that held the hat above the head.

Self-tipping Hat
A gentleman in 1896 tipped his hat when he met a lady, but what if his hands were full of bundles? J.C. Boyle invented a hat that tipped itself when the wearer bowed slightly forward!

Device for Measuring Heads
In 1879 a hatter of Paris ensured a perfect fit with his "hat conformator." It pricked out a paper pattern of a customer's head shape.

Helmet for Shipwrecks
In 1878 Francis P. Cumberford devised a rubber helmet with glass eye windows. A rubber speaking trumpet was included, which would amplify the victim's calls for help.

Helmet with Solar-powered Cooling Fan
Available today, this hat is perfect for people who work or play in the sun. A solar-powered fan provides built-in air conditioning!

On Your Own

Invent a hat that performs at least three different functions. Draw a diagram of your creation. Who would wear it? What would you call it?

Answers

Fouled-up Fix-it Shoppe

What a mess! Can you help repair all the broken items?

t often takes many different parts—working together—to make something function correctly. The fan in this picture has a broken blade. Until it's repaired it just won't work! It's a good thing that the owner of the fan took it to this fix-it shop! Or is it? There are lots of things that need repairing here. The parts are ready and waiting—but everything is all mixed up.

Somebody needs to get this place organized! Examine the numbered items in the picture. Each needs a new part to replace a broken or missing one. Can you find the correct parts? Match each broken item with the location of the part needed to repair it.

○ The part needed is on a shelf.
△ The part needed is in a drawer.
□ The part needed is on the floor.

Instead of ending up in a trash can, all of the broken items listed below have been repaired. That means their owners can get a lot more use out of them. You can see that by fixing one small part, the whole can often be saved!

fan

blade

$15.00

skateboard

wheel

$3.50

bicycle

pedal

$7.50

grand-
father clock

pendulum

$25.00

toaster

cord and

plug

$6.50

pencil

sharpener

handle

$2.50

fishing rod

reel

$7.50

lawn
mower

set of
blades

$9.00

record
player

arm

$10.00

guitar

neck

$10.00

On Your Own

Look around your home and make a list of items that need repair. Find out where you would take these things to have them fixed. Hint: Check the Yellow Pages for names and addresses of specific repair shops.

Answers

Key in on the Problem

Help the novice locksmith make perfect spare keys for his customers.

eople have used locks for many centuries. But before an American, Linus Yale, Jr., invented his modern lock and key system in 1865, locks were easily picked open. To solve this problem, Yale invented locks and keys with special grooves cut in them. He made each lock and key set unique. Finally, people could keep their valuables safely locked up without fear of burglars!

Look at the picture to the right. Customers have brought their keys to the locksmith's shop to have spare copies made. Because the locksmith is new on the job, not every key he makes will work. Can you tell which of the spare keys he's made are perfect copies and which are not?

Examine the ten numbered original keys in the upper part of the picture. Then look at the spare keys below. For each original key, decide if:

○ A perfect match has been made.

□ A perfect match has not been made.

8

Ancient Egyptian wooden key

Ancient Greek key

Ancient Roman keys

How the Yale Lock Works

The history of lockmaking took a dramatic turn with the invention of Yale's pin-tumbler lock, shown here. This was an entirely new kind of lock and was the first to be mass produced. Yale's name is known in many countries even today and his lock is used in more doors than any other kind of lock.

Modern key

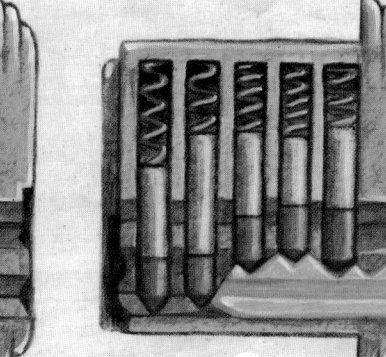

1   2

This side view of the Yale lock shows (1) the pins in the locked position and (2) the grooves on the key raising the pins, which free the key to turn, and unlock the door. (If the key does not have just the right grooves, the pins do not line up properly and the key cannot turn.)

Another advantage of Yale's modern lock system is that it replaced the giant-sized "skeleton" keys of previous times with smaller, flatter keys like the ones we use today. The collection of ancient keys on this page shows how keys have changed through the ages.

German key of the 1600's

Italian key of the 1500's

Bronze keys from the Middle Ages

On Your Own

On a large piece of plain paper, trace all the keys your family members use. Are any of the grooved patterns similar? To test your own inventiveness, devise some type of system for quickly telling one key from another. Try out your system on different family members to see if they find their keys faster by using your system.

Answers

Crime-busting Inventions

Use your wits to solve this million-dollar museum art heist.

ears ago detectives like Sherlock Holmes scoured the scenes of crimes with only a magnifying glass and a bloodhound to sniff for clues. Modern detectives, though, use whole laboratories full of scientific equipment to help them solve crimes. High-speed computers, laser scanners, and sound spectrographs are among the high-tech tools at their disposal.

Now here's a crime for you to solve: A valuable painting has been stolen from a famous museum. A mysterious caller has demanded a ransom of one million dollars in exchange for the safe return of the painting. But who's the culprit?

Each of the six suspects at the right has a police record for art theft. Study their appearances and examine their police records. Then use clues 1 through 9 to conclude "whodunit" in question 10.

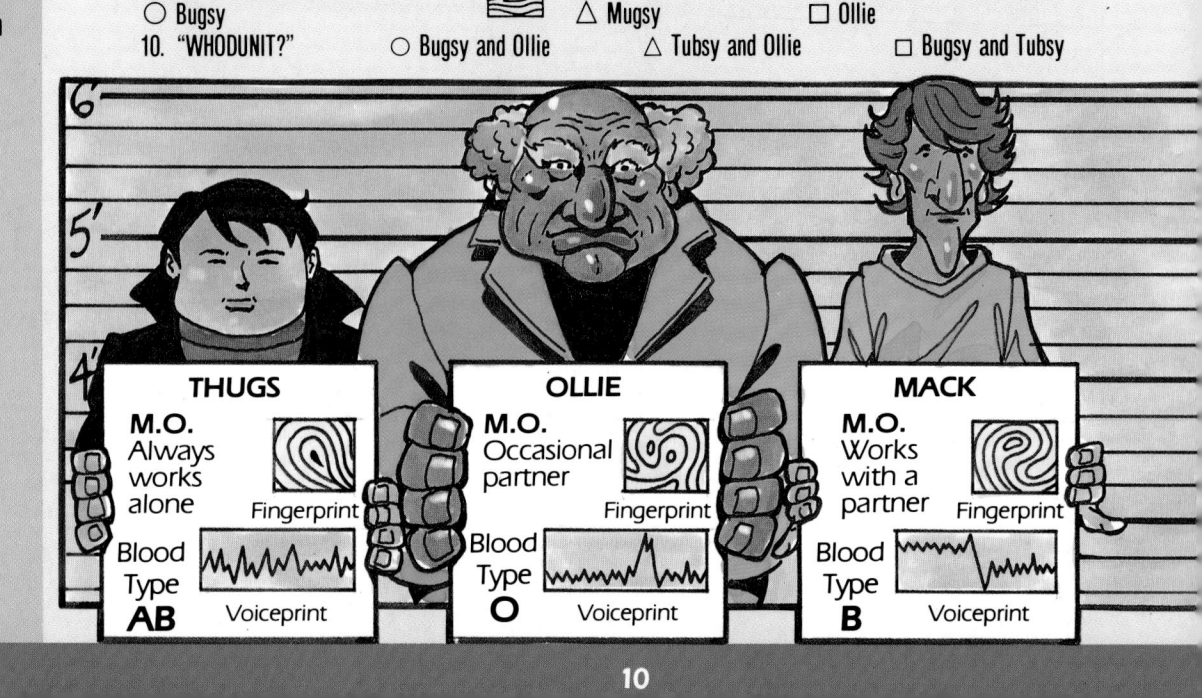

MUGSY
M.O. Always works alone
Fingerprint
Blood Type **A**
Voiceprint

BUGSY
M.O. Sometimes has a partner
Fingerprint
Blood Type **O**
Voiceprint

TUBSY
M.O. Always has a partner
Fingerprint
Blood Type **A**
Voiceprint

CLUES

1. A witness saw a man with a big nose, bushy eyebrows, and a thick lower lip fleeing the scene. Who could it be?
   ○ Mugsy, Bugsy, Tubsy, or Thugs △ Mugsy, Bugsy, Tubsy, or Ollie □ Mugsy, Bugsy, Tubsy, or Mack
2. A strand of blond hair is found at the crime scene. Who's a suspect?
   ○ Bugsy, Tubsy, and Mack △ Bugsy, Tubsy, and Thugs □ Bugsy, Tubsy, and Ollie
3. A microscope reveals the hair in clue #2 is curly. Who's suspect now?
   ○ Tubsy and Mugsy △ Tubsy and Ollie □ Mack and Ollie
4. A footprint outside the museum back door implicates which two tall, very heavy suspects?
   ○ Tubsy and Ollie △ Bugsy and Tubsy □ Bugsy and Ollie
5. BREAKTHROUGH! This suspect's voiceprint matches the voiceprint ( ) taken during the ransom call.
   ○ Ollie △ Tubsy □ Bugsy
6. The police record of the suspect identified by clue #5 shows he works with a partner. Who could it be?
   ○ Mack, Ollie, or Thugs △ Bugsy, Mack, or Ollie □ Bugsy, Mugsy, or Ollie
7. A green thread found on a nail by the back door points to which suspects?
   ○ Bugsy, Ollie, and Thugs △ Mack, Ollie, and Thugs □ Bugsy, Mack, and Ollie
8. Traces of blood type O were also found on the nail. Who's still suspect?
   ○ Bugsy and Ollie △ Bugsy and Thugs □ Bugsy and Mack
9. BREAKTHROUGH! This fingerprint ( ) on the back door identifies which suspect as the accomplice?
   ○ Bugsy △ Mugsy □ Ollie
10. "WHODUNIT?" ○ Bugsy and Ollie △ Tubsy and Ollie □ Bugsy and Tubsy

THUGS
M.O. Always works alone
Fingerprint
Blood Type **AB**
Voiceprint

OLLIE
M.O. Occasional partner
Fingerprint
Blood Type **O**
Voiceprint

MACK
M.O. Works with a partner
Fingerprint
Blood Type **B**
Voiceprint

Find books in the library about fingerprinting and other crime investigation techniques. Study the four main types of fingerprints. Use an ink pad or water-base marker to make finger-prints of your family members and friends. Label each fingerprint with its type.

Visit a modern crime lab:

A. The **Ident-o-kit** helps the police artist sketch a suspect's different facial features from witnesses' descriptions of a suspect.

B. The **comparison microscope** can analyze both color and texture of even a single strand of hair and compare it with a suspect's hair.

C. The **X-ray diffractometer** can match dirt on a suspect's shoe with dirt at the crime scene.

D. The **sound spectrograph** makes a voiceprint, which is as unique to each person as his or her fingerprint.

E. The **high-speed crime computer** files the police records on known criminals, including their methods of operation (M.O.).

F. The **scanning electron microscope** can reveal information about even the tiniest thread from a suspect's clothing.

G. **Serology tests** identify the criminal's blood type from traces of blood.

H. The new **portable laser scanner** can be taken to the crime scene to detect even the faintest fingerprints.

Wheelin' Along

Imagine you have X-ray vision. Hook up your superhuman eyes and try to see which of these objects contain hidden wheels inside.

 rom the log roller to the Lunar Rover, the wheel has been the most useful invention ever created. No one is sure who invented the wheel, but it has changed the way things work and move since its introduction about 5000 years ago.

What would our world be like without the wheel? We wouldn't have bicycles, cars, buses, trains, planes, skateboards, tractors and so many more of the vehicles we use. But not all items with wheels are forms of transportation. Some objects have wheels at work on the inside where you can't see them. Without these internal wheels, the machines wouldn't work. Don't forget that gears are wheels, too.

Use your X-ray vision to decide which of the ten listed items on this page have hidden wheels inside and which objects do not have hidden wheels inside.

○ Has inner wheels at work
□ Has no wheels inside

1. Escalator
2. Coffee maker (electric)
3. Food mixer
4. Speedometer
5. Clock
6. Aerosol paint can
7. Ballpoint pen
8. Flashlight
9. Traffic signal
10. Elevator

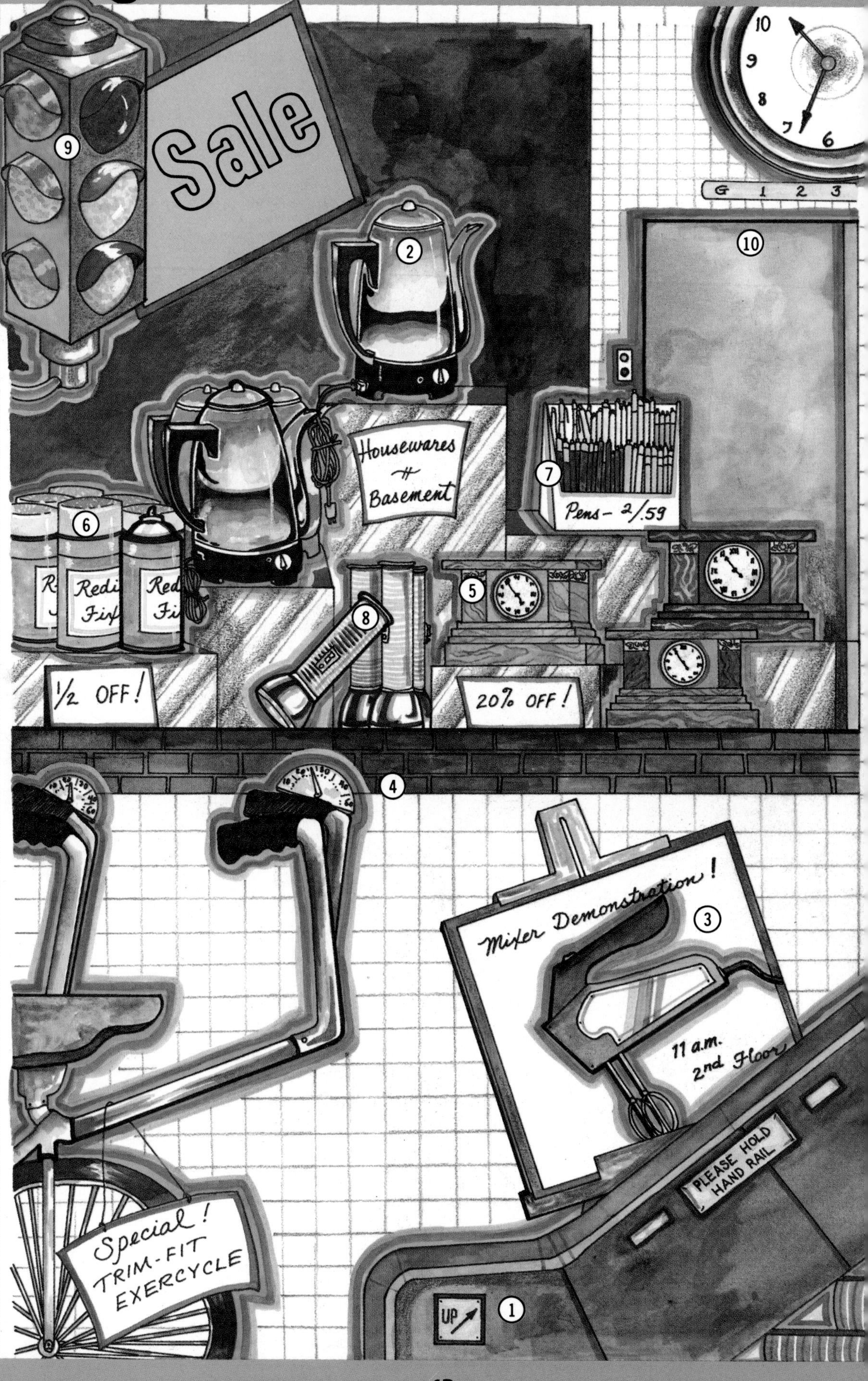

12

Use these cut-away drawings to check the accuracy of your X-ray vision. You may have to look very carefully to detect the hidden wheels in these items.

Unless you really do have X-ray eyes, it is almost impossible to know what's going on inside a machine. It is often true, though, that if a machine moves from one place to another, or if it moves something from one place to another, it has wheels inside. (Remember, a wheel is a round object that rotates on an axis at its center.)

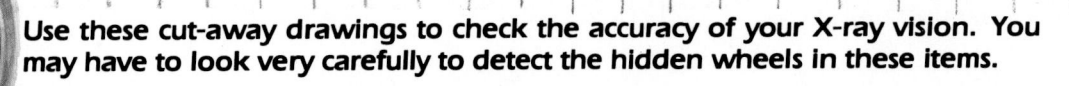

Escalators move people from one floor to another. Look inside the escalator on this page. You can see the wheels that make the escalator move. Now look at the elevator at the bottom of this page. The wheels above the elevator turn to lift the elevator cable.

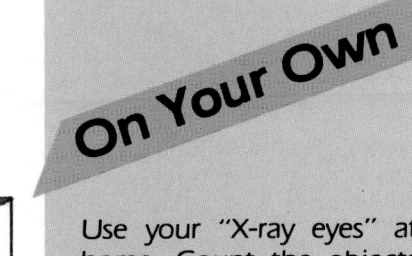

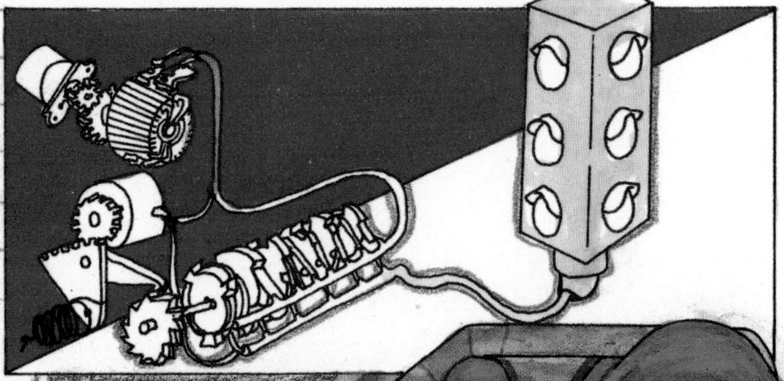

The inside of a clock contains wheels that turn the hands of the clock. Wheels also turn the beaters of the mixer around and around. Gears, or toothed wheels, transmit the speed of a vehicle to a shaft connected with a mechanism that moves a pointer on the dial of a speedometer.

From the outside, it might not seem as though a traffic signal moves at all. Inside, however, many different wheels control the timing device and light switches.

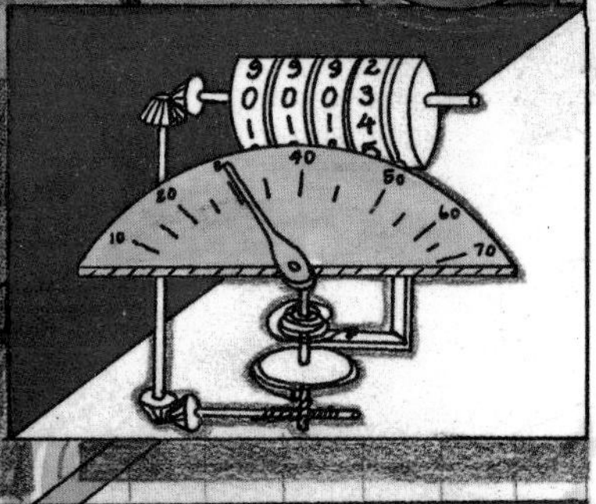

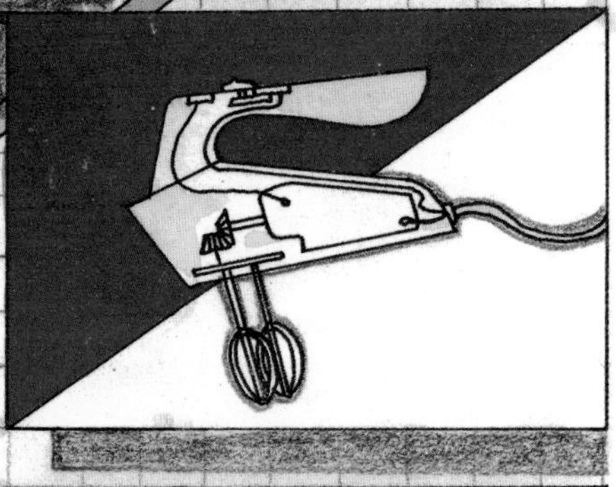

The aerosol can, coffee maker, ballpoint pen and flashlight have other machine parts that make them work, but they do not have wheels.

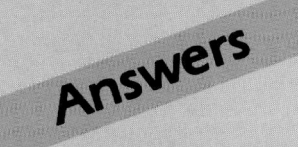

On Your Own

Use your "X-ray eyes" at home. Count the objects you think might have hidden wheels inside. Find a cast-off object that you think might have hidden wheels, get adult permission, and take the object apart to see what's inside. Keep these parts in a special box for future projects.

Answers

Crazy Contraptions

Too much work to do around the house? Combine these simple machines to help you get the job done!

ave you ever used a machine that made a big deal out of a simple task? Inventors sometimes get carried away with their ideas, adding details to machines that should be kept simple.

The picture on the right shows one such machine. Though made of many different parts, it was actually designed to perform just one specific job. Is all this work really worth the bother? Answer the questions on this page and decide for yourself.

1. **What action starts the machine working?**
   ○ The skate rolls down the piece of wood.
   △ The boy turns the crank on the jack-in-the-box.
   □ The jack-in-the-box's head hits the piece of wood.

2. **Which part of the machine acts as a pulley?**
   ○ B   △ A   □ D

3. **What is the job of the wedge in the machine?**
   ○ To lift the cat
   △ To cut the watermelon
   □ To move the roller skate

4. **Which part of the machine works as an inclined plane?**
   ○ D   △ F   □ B

5. **Which part works by means of a spring?**
   ○ D   △ E   □ G

6. **Which of these machine parts contain wheels?**
   ○ A and D   △ A and G   □ Only A

7. **What is the job of the lever and fulcrum in this machine?**
   ○ To raise the cat
   △ To release the jack-in-the-box
   □ To hold the water balloon

8. **What happens last in this machine?**
   ○ The water balloon descends.
   △ The water balloon hits the cactus and breaks.
   □ The cat cuts the rope with the scissors.

9. **In what order do things happen in this machine?**
   ○ C E F A B G D
   △ C A E F B G D
   □ G D C E F A B

10. **This machine works in 7 steps. The last step finally does the job the machine was designed to do. Just what is this crazy contraption?**
    ○ A watermelon-slicing machine
    △ A rope-cutting machine
    □ A cactus-watering machine

The contraption on the left-hand page is really a combination of many simple machines. Let's look at them separately.

An **inclined plane** is a flat surface that is slanted. Ramps are inclined planes that help us move things more easily. The inclined plane in our crazy contraption helps the roller skate move faster.

The axe that cuts the watermelon is a **wedge.** A wedge is a piece of wood or metal that is tapered at one end. It is then pounded into an object (like wood) to split or cut it.

You may call it a seesaw, but the cat in the picture is really sitting on a **lever and fulcrum.** A lever is a machine that helps lift things. The fulcrum is the support on which a lever rests.

A **pulley** is a simple machine made up of a rope or cable and a grooved wheel. Several pulleys together can make lifting heavy loads much easier.

Wheels are part of many machines. Our wacky invention uses them on the roller skate, the pulley, and the gears inside the jack-in-the-box. You use wheels every day, on bicycles, cars, toys, and much more.

A **spring** is an elastic device that returns to its original shape after being released. When the lid of the jack-in-the-box opens, the spring is released and the toy doll pops up.

On Your Own

A cartoonist named Rube Goldberg became famous for creating absurdly complicated machines to do very simple tasks. Look up some of Goldberg's contraptions. Then design a contraption of your own to do a simple job, like making your bed.

Answers

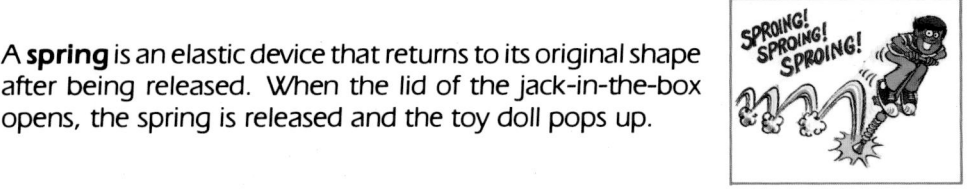

The Magic of Invention

Expand your powers of imagination as you soar from inspiration to invention!

An inventor's mind can leap from old and familiar things to new and wondrous ones. Ben Franklin, for example, saw lightning and imagined the possibilities of electricity. The Wright Brothers played with kites and made the dream of a flying machine come true. These leaps of imagination changed history.

Can you see with an inventor's eye? Look at the numbered items to the left of the magician. Each of these items inspired one of the inventions coming out of the hat. Put your imagination to work and match inspiration to invention!

1. Rubber bottle
   ○ H   □ A
2. Rubber ball
   ○ J   □ A
3. Hobby horse
   ○ B   □ C
4. Piano
   ○ D   □ E
5. Paper tube
   ○ H   □ I
6. Railroad
   ○ D   □ I
7. Windmill
   ○ C   □ D
8. Bellows
   ○ G   □ I
9. Ferry boat
   ○ A   □ G
10. Folding chairs
   ○ F   □ B

■ "Inspiration hit me right be-tween the eyes," said grocer Sylvan Goldman. He put two folding chairs, baskets, and four wheels to-gether and invented the shopping cart in 1936.

■ In the 1500's Leonardo da Vinci took the concept of a windmill, added a power source, and designed the first helicopter. But it wasn't until 1919 that technology produced a working model.

■ In 1820 Thomas Hancock thought of a new use for rubber bottles. He sliced them up into bands and used them to make garters and waist-bands. Stephen Perry saw the endless possibilities of the product and opened the first rubber band factory in England in 1845.

■ While watching bellows fan a fire, C.J. Harvey thought about reversing the process. He eventually invented the first machine for sucking in dirt. We call it the vacuum cleaner!

■ Dr. Rene Laennec had trouble hearing a clear heartbeat in some of his patients. Seeing children play with a board and a stick, he remembered that matter carried sound better than air. Laennec rolled a piece of paper into a tube and listened to a patient's chest. The first stethoscope was born!

■ The hobby horse was propelled by foot and moved rather slowly on four wheels. In contrast, the two-wheeled bicycle that it later inspired moved swiftly and easily. It has remained relatively unchanged for the last 100 years.

■ In the 1860's many people tried to invent a writing machine. Watching a pianist, Christopher Sholes was inspired to use a system of keys which struck a metal letter-and-roller combination. The typewriter was invented!

■ While waiting for the Staten Island ferry one day, Schuyler Wheeler thought that if a wheel could move water it could move air as well. He set his idea to work and invented the electric fan.

■ Europeans first saw rubber when they found Indians of South and Central America bouncing rubber balls. In 1819 a Scotsman, Charles Macintosh, discovered a way to dissolve rubber. He designed the first rubber-coated raincoat, and called it a "macintosh."

■ Railroad trains move on a horizontal track. Elisha Graves Otis visualized a track that could carry things vertically, also. By 1854 he designed a version of the elevator with a built-in safety device that held the elevator in place even if the lifting cable was cut.

On Your Own

Roll a sheet of paper into a tube. Use it to listen to a friend's heartbeat, noise through a wall, and the tick-ing of a clock. Can you hear better using the tube than without it?

Answers

Back to Nature

Look at nature with an inventor's eye! Can you see the possibilities?

Human beings are great inventors, but Mother Nature often did it first! Would it surprise you to learn that many of the inventions we use every day were copied directly from things in nature?

Look at the picture to the right. At some time in the past, someone looked at each of the various things in this nature garden and became inspired to invent something. Examine the numbered items carefully. Then decide from the list below which human invention each of them inspired.

1. ○ Zipper   □ Velcro
2. ○ Shoes   □ Baby rattle
3. ○ Paper money   □ Tent
4. ○ Toothbrush   □ Barbed wire
5. ○ Syrup   □ Chewing gum
6. ○ Flyswatter   □ Bear trap
7. ○ Vacuum cleaner hose   □ Flexible pressurized suit
8. ○ Powder puff   □ Parachute
9. ○ Synthetic fiber   □ Drinking straw
10. ○ Flashlight   □ Sound and light show

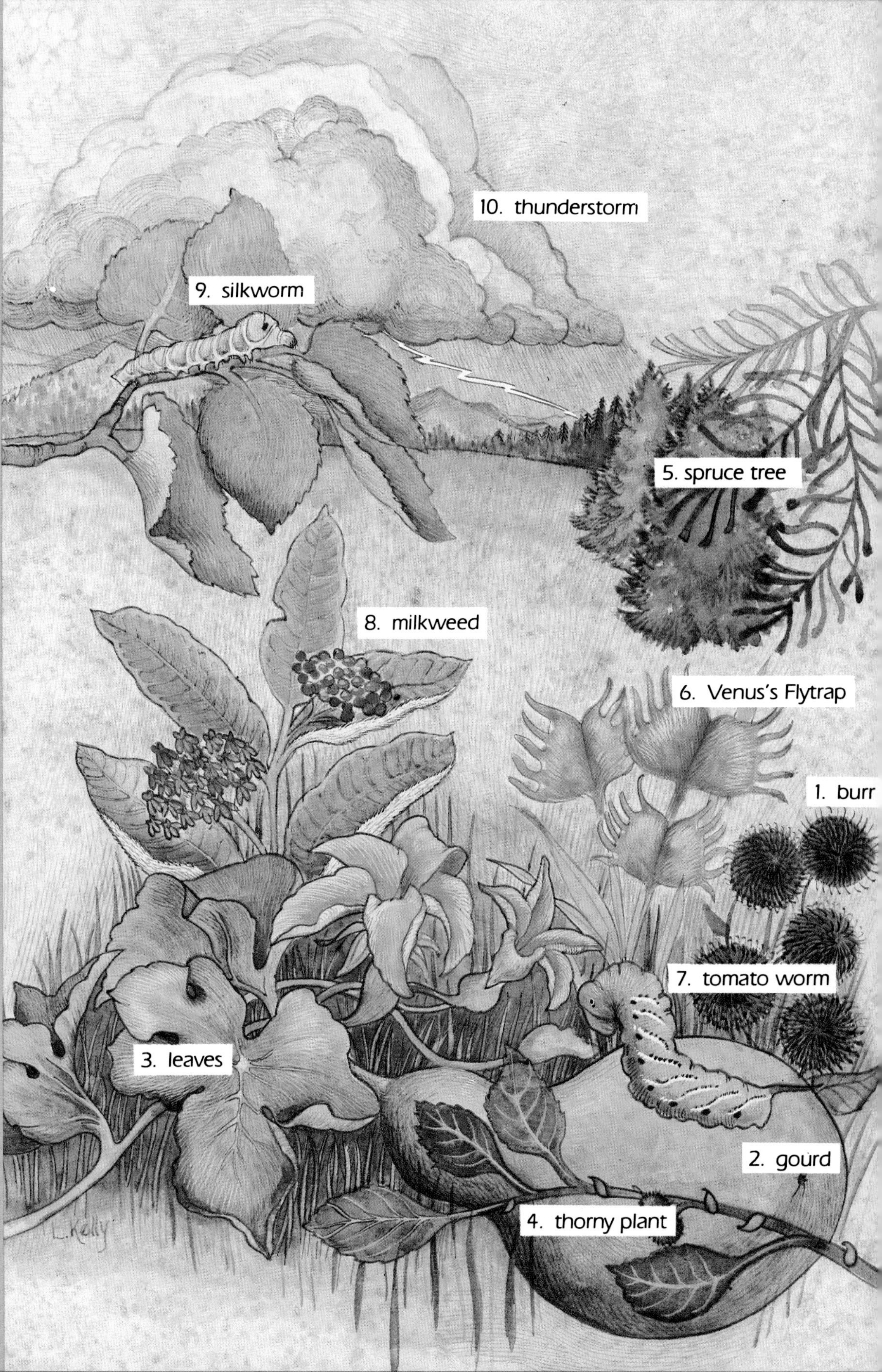

10. thunderstorm

9. silkworm

5. spruce tree

8. milkweed

6. Venus's Flytrap

1. burr

7. tomato worm

3. leaves

2. gourd

4. thorny plant

L. Kelly

Settlers in the American West planted thorny shrubs, like osage orange, to keep their livestock from roaming. These "natural" fences inspired Joseph F. Glidden to develop barbed wire—twisted steel wire containing thornlike barbs.

Wiley Post, one of the first round-the-world aviators, wanted to set high altitude records as well. He designed a pressurized flight suit, but it was awkward to wear. One day he watched a tomato worm crawling on a plant. This gave him the idea to sew flexible sections into the joints of his pressurized suit to make it more comfortable.

Benjamin Franklin was assigned to a committee responsible for printing money during the Revolutionary War. Observing that the veins of leaves are never exactly alike, he suggested printing a leaf design on the paper currency to make it difficult to copy.

It is quite possible that the umbrella-shaped fluffy seeds of the milkweed led to the development of the parachute. Man-made parachutes have holes in their canopies for better steering. The milkweed is composed of separate tufts. This allows air to pass through it, giving milkweeds the ability to travel great distances.

After a walk, George De Mestral struggled to remove burrs from his clothing and from his dog. He later examined one of the burrs under a microscope and discovered that it contained tiny hooks that easily attached to fur—or to his own clothing. Eight years later De Mestral invented Velcro. Like the burr, each Velcro strip contains thousands of tiny hooks! When pressed together, the strips fasten and hold tightly.

Long sticky fibers spun by the silkworm inspired the development of man-made fibers such as nylon, rayon, and dacron. In fact, in 1884 Hilaire Chardonnet patented the first practical synthetic fiber and called it artificial silk.

When shaken, dried gourds produce a rattling sound. The colorful rattles babies play with today can be traced to the gourds primitive people used as rattles and drums.

Try to catch a bug by cupping your two hands together. The Venus's-flytrap plant catches flies in much the same way. Metal bear traps operate on this same principle, too.

In 1939 Paul Robert-Houdin stared in wonder at a nearby castle lit up by a violent thunderstorm. The flashes of lightning and thunderous noise created a dramatic show! This experience—and the later invention of stereophonic sound—led Robert-Houdin to produce the first "sound and light show" in 1953. Since then, exciting sound and light shows have been produced at the pyramids of Egypt and the Acropolis in Athens.

Like other foresters of the mid-19th century, John B. Curtis chewed the sap, or gum, that seeps from spruce trees. But he also tried something different—cooking the sap and adding flavors. John B. Curtis sold his concoction in wrapped sticks, called it "State of Maine Pure Spruce Gum," and made a small fortune!

On Your Own

Leaf rubbings are like fingerprints—no two are alike. Prove this for yourself! Choose three or four leaves that appear to look the same. Cover each leaf with a sheet of paper and rub thoroughly with the side of a crayon. Compare your results.

Answers

Leonardo, Artist of Invention

Decode the ideas of one of the most brilliant inventors of all time.

Leonardo da Vinci (1452-1519) was a world-famous artist, but he was also a genius of invention. He used his artistic vision and vivid imagination to design hundreds of things. Many of his ideas were turned into inventions long after he drew them. Others were never developed.

To the right are ten sketches redrawn from Leonardo's notebooks. These sketches show ideas that were eventually turned into real working inventions. Read the list of inventions below. Then choose the letter of the sketch that matches each invention.

1. Clock
   ○ E   △ G   □ J
2. Diving snorkel
   ○ H   △ I   □ E
3. Armored car
   ○ A   △ B   □ D
4. Projector
   ○ J   △ G   □ A
5. Spinning wheel
   ○ C   △ H   □ J
6. Helicopter
   ○ F   △ C   □ B
7. Paddle wheel boat
   ○ C   △ B   □ A
8. Parachute
   ○ B   △ F   □ A
9. Movable crane
   ○ H   △ I   □ E
10. Automobile
   ○ A   △ B   □ D

Leonardo da Vinci often recorded his notes in an unusual way—he wrote backwards! Try to decipher each of the words written backwards on this page. Then read some facts about Leonardo's "ahead-of-their-time" ideas.

On Your Own

Many inventions start as simple sketches long before they are actually made. Sketch your idea of a new invention, whether or not it can work in exactly the way you've drawn it. Describe what it can do and how it is to be used.

- provided a floating air supply on the water surface
- allowed diver to stay under water for a long time

- was regarded as first helicopter
- was forerunner of modern propeller

- registered minutes and hours
- had two clock faces, each moved by a weighted cord and gears

- was an improvement of earlier boat design
- needed no oars

- was hundreds of years ahead of its time
- was designed to carry cannons inside body of tank

- designed as a closed linen tent, similar to today's parachute, for getting down from high places

- allowed spinning and winding to be done at same time
- made spinning easier and quicker

- allowed a candle-lit object to cast a picture on paper
- used same principle as in modern projectors

- was spring-driven for continuous motion
- has worked successfully when made as a model automobile

- moved on a wheel and was guided by overhead cable
- could lift and lower load when handle of crane was turned

Answers

21

Mechanical Marvels

Sure, robots are talented . . . but are they really this talented?

obots have been designed to do some amazing things since they were introduced in the 1920's. Lots of books and movies show robots that look human. In real life, though, most robots look more like machines than people.

It used to be thought that robots could only perform very simple tasks, but new advances in the science of robotics have enabled these mechanical marvels to do a variety of complex jobs.

Ten job openings are listed in the Employment Office at the right. Which of these ten jobs could be performed by robots as well as humans? Read each numbered job description and decide if:

○ Robots are now able to do this job.

☐ Robots are not able to do this job yet.

1 **Welder** To weld 1,000 auto frames per day	6 **Baby Sitter** To give warm loving care to small children
2 **Nurse Helper** To deliver medicine to hospital patients	7 **Underwater Explorer** To seek out treasure
3 **Brain Surgeon** To perform delicate surgery	8 **Rock Musician** To "groove out" on a large console organ
4 **Calligraphy Artist** To paint letters with a brush	9 **Space Geologist** To dig up and analyze Martian soil
5 **Ice Sculptor** To carve shimmering ice statues	10 **Robot Builder** To assemble robots

Robot is a Czechoslovakian word that means "worker." It was first used as a term for working machines by Karel Capek in his 1920 play, <u>RUR,</u> or <u>Rossum's Universal Robots.</u> Many people at that time were afraid of robots, thinking they would harm people and take jobs from them. Today we know that robots help make our lives better by performing tasks too dangerous, difficult, or repetitive for humans.

Soon robots will be able to do just about everything people can do. They'll never replace human parents, families, friends, and caregivers, though. No machine can ever love you the way a human can.

Your local library has many exciting books on robots, both new and old. Try to find pictures of the earliest computers and robots. How do they compare with the newest robot designs? Design your own robot. What will it look like? What is its name?

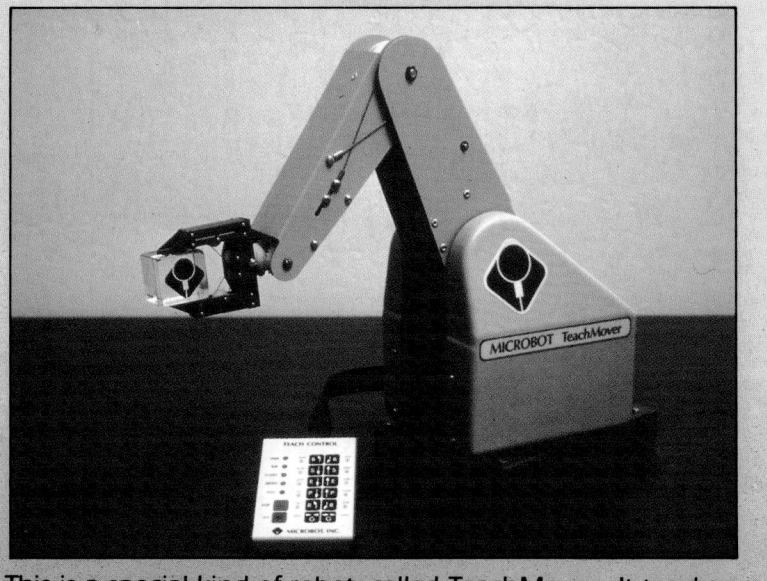

This is a special kind of robot, called TeachMover. It teaches students all about robotics, the science of designing and using robots. Its "intelligent" gripper "fingers" can judge whether or not they're holding an object. The robotic arm can twist and bend at least five different ways at once. It can rotate on its base, bend its "shoulder," bend its "elbow," bend its "wrist" up and down, and twist its "wrist" from side to side.

Because TeachMover's built-in microcomputer can remember up to 53 complete positions, students can make the arm move in many complex, step-by-step patterns. Perhaps your school will someday have a teaching robot such as this. If you could program it to do whatever you want, what would you ask TeachMover to do for you?

Edison's Bright Ideas

Follow this maze of cords for an electrifying adventure!

homas Alva Edison has been called the greatest inventor the world has ever known. His inventions have changed millions of lives. Would it surprise you to learn that many of his inventions were actually improvements of existing things? Much of Edison's genius was his ability to take something and make it better. Above all, he tried to develop things people really needed. Even the light bulb, for which he is so famous, was not his original idea. Edison, however, improved light bulbs so that for the first time they could be used in people's homes—where they were needed!

All of the modern electrical inventions illustrated on this page were either invented or improved in some way by Edison. Look at the picture to the right. Follow the electrical cord from each invention to its correct plug outlet. Decide whether each cord is:

○ In good working order and properly plugged into an outlet

△ In good working order but not plugged into an outlet

□ In need of repair

1. Movie projector
2. Lamp
3. Radio
4. Phonograph
5. Motion picture camera
6. Stock ticker
7. Telephone
8. Microphone
9. Typewriter
10. Ceiling lamp

1) A classroom in Michigan, 1854 . . .

Tom Edison was always asking questions—questions that usually began with **why** or **how**.

Why does water put out fire?

You're wasting my time, Tom! Just be quiet and listen!

In his first weeks at school, his teacher decided that he was "addled."

2) His mother took him out of school after only 3 months. She was certain that he could learn better at home.

Do you really want to know **why** and **how** things happen, Tom? Experiment! Search out answers for yourself!

Mrs. Edison encouraged Tom to go as far as his curiosity could take him.

3) At age 9 Tom tested every experiment in a chemistry book—to try and prove the author wrong!

At age 12 he printed his own newspaper.

At age 16 he was a telegraph operator.

Whatever he was doing, Tom Edison was always tinkering with something new!

4) The first invention he tried to sell was a vote-recording machine. With high hopes he took it to the U.S. Congress.

Congressman, Sir, with this invention you can record your votes more quickly.

Sorry, my boy. It takes us 45 minutes to vote by roll call. We like to have that time to trade votes. We just don't **need** your invention.

Tom vowed that he'd never again waste time on things nobody wanted.

5) From then on he worked tirelessly on what he called the "desperate needs of the world."

Tom, you've tried about 10,000 versions of that contraption. Isn't that enough failure for you?

I haven't failed, my friend. I've just found 10,000 ways that don't work.

6) But Tom Edison made hundreds of things that worked very well. Among them:

the first practical electrical light bulb—

the first phonograph—

one of the earliest motion picture cameras—

Thomas Alva Edison patented more than 1,100 inventions before his death in 1931.

On Your Own

Thomas Edison has often been called a genius. Edison himself defined genius as being "one percent inspiration and 99 percent perspiration." What did he mean by this? How could this saying apply to things that you do in your own life?

Answers

What's in a Name?

Creating an invention is one challenge; giving it a name is another! Discover how some well-known inventions got their names.

 ave you ever heard of the I-Scream-Bar? It's not likely, because its inventor, Chester Nelson, soon changed this product's name to something else. The I-Scream-Bar was the world's first candy-coated ice cream bar. Nelson wanted his product's name to make people think of something cold and sweet. He was afraid that I-Scream just didn't do the job. His new name choice? The Eskimo Pie!

What's in a name? Plenty! A well-chosen name can help sell a product or invention. (The Eskimo Pie has been a success for more than sixty years.) A lackluster name can leave people confused or uninterested.

A name can be chosen for many reasons. But any invention's name should say something about the product—something that helps people remember it!

The picture to the right shows ten inventions. You are probably familiar with most of their names. But do you know the origins of these names? Look at each numbered invention and decide if it:

○ Has a descriptive name (tells what it looks like, what it is made of, or how it works)
△ Is named after someone
□ Both ○ and △

1. Zipper

3. Zeppelin

6. Ferris Wheel

9. Thermos Bottle

10. Sandwich

4. Saxophone

8. Automobile

7. Teddy Bear

5. Aqualung

2. Submarine

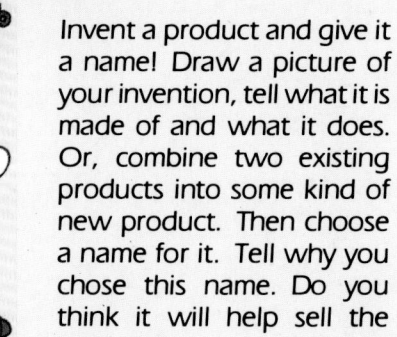

◻ Its inventors called it a "hookless fastener." Upon seeing the device demonstrated on a pair of boots; an impressed executive at B.F. Goodrich said, "Zip 'er up!" The name stuck.

◻ Adolphe Sax was trying to improve the bass clarinet. Instead, he invented the saxophone. The instrument quickly became popular in military bands. Today, the saxophone is used to play all kinds of music, from jazz to rock to classical.

◻ A submarine is a ship that sails underwater. (Sub means under, marine means water.) The first functioning submarine was made by Cornelius van Drebbel in 1620. It was made of wood and leather and was propelled by 12 rowers.

◻ John Montague loved to play cards. Once, after playing all day and all night, he got hungry. He didn't want to leave the game, so he told his servants to bring him some meat between two pieces of bread. John and his friends thought that it was a wonderful way to eat, and the idea soon caught on. We can, therefore, thank John Montague, Earl of Sandwich, for one of our favorite food items today.

◻ In its early years it was often called a "horseless carriage," but its official name was, and still is, the automobile. (Auto means self, mobile means moving.)

◻ What amusement park ride measured 250 feet in diameter and could carry over 2,000 people high into the air for a spectacular view? It was the incredible Ferris wheel built for the 1893 Columbian Exhibition in Chicago. This gigantic creation held 36 glass viewing cars, each of which could carry 60 people! Modern Ferris wheels are far more modest, but they still carry the name of their inventor, G.W. Gale Ferris.

◻ In 1942 Jacques Cousteau and Emile Gagnan invented the aqualung. (Aqua means water.) With this device divers could carry their air supply down into the ocean with them; they no longer had to be attached by air hoses to the surface.

◻ The zeppelin was an ancestor of the modern-day blimp. These huge airships were built in the early 1900's and carried passengers and mail, just as airlines do today. The zeppelin was named after its creator, Ferdinand von Zeppelin.

◻ The teddy bear got its name from President Theodore Roosevelt's son, Teddy. The young boy, grief-stricken over the loss of a live pet bear, was given a cloth bear as a gift. Today, furry toy bears are called teddy bears the world over.

◻ Have you ever carried hot soup in a thermos bottle? If you have, you know that the thermos keeps hot food nice and warm. It's not surprising, then, that thermos is the Greek word for hot!

Invent a product and give it a name! Draw a picture of your invention, tell what it is made of and what it does. Or, combine two existing products into some kind of new product. Then choose a name for it. Tell why you chose this name. Do you think it will help sell the product?

Answers

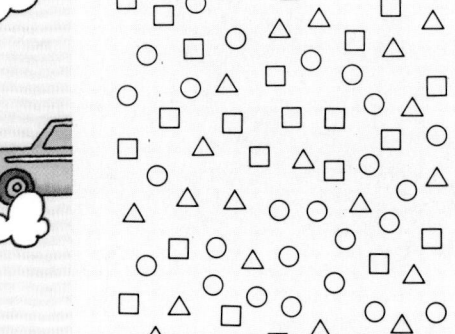

Was It Discovered . . . or Invented?

Share the excitement of new finds!

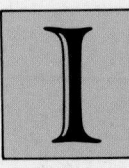In 1849 prospectors shouted, "Aha! There's gold in California!" They had uncovered something that had always been there, but no one had seen it before. They had discovered gold.

Scientific concepts, such as gravity, are also said to be discovered. When laws of nature—that have always existed—are understood for the first time, they are called discoveries.

Inventors also shout "Aha!" when they put ideas and materials together to make something that wasn't there before. Whether it is brand new, or an improvement of an older idea, it is still called an invention.

Here's a list of things people have shouted "Aha!" about throughout history. Some are discoveries. Others are inventions. Can you tell which are which?

○ It was discovered.
□ It was invented.

1. Paper
2. Halley's comet
3. Rubber eraser
4. Kaleidoscope
5. X-ray
6. Dynamite
7. Magnetism
8. Windshield wipers
9. Penicillin
10. Silk

M Rich

Here are some thoughts that might have come from the notebooks of inventors and discoverers as they exclaimed "Aha!"

Aha! I've been studying some new material that comes from trees in South America. I discovered that the substance can rub out pencil marks. Maybe it should be called rubber!
Joseph Priestley   1770

Aha! I've invented a window cleaning device. When rain or snow gets on the windshield of an automobile or trolley, the driver can turn a handle to move a rubber blade. Much safer!
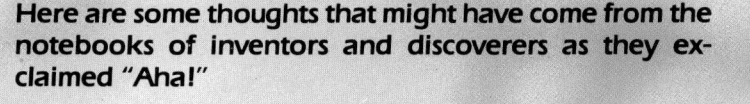
Mary Anderson   1903

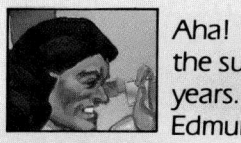

Aha! I've discovered the orbit of the "Great Comet" around the sun! I now predict that it will reappear about every 77 years.
Edmund Halley   1682

Aha! By working with compasses and lodestones, I've discovered that the Earth is a great magnet! That's why a compass needle points north and south to the two poles!
William Gilbert   1600

Aha! A mold appeared in the culture of common germs I was studying. This penicillium mold stops the growth of bacteria. It should be useful in fighting diseases.
Alexander Fleming   1928

Aha! I experimented with the inner bark of the mulberry tree. I broke some into fibers and pounded them into a sheet. I find it excellent for writing on with brush and ink!
Ts'ai Lun   105 A.D.

Aha! While I was doing an experiment with electric current, I discovered rays that passed through most substances, but not through metal or bone! I think they can be used for medical diagnosis. I call them X rays.
Wilhelm Conrad Roentgen   1895

Aha! Last week, as I drank tea under the mulberry trees, a caterpillar cocoon fell into my cup! It had a loose fiber. I unwound it and discovered a strong thread, about half a mile long! I had some woven into silk cloth. Beautiful!
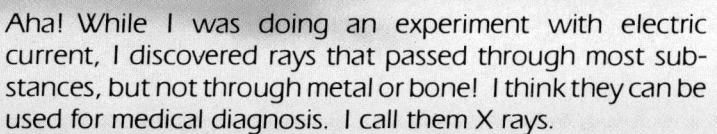
Empress Si Ling-chi   2640 B.C.

Aha! I have invented a safe blasting material. The old explosive, nitroglycerine, could be very dangerous. I used it to make dynamite, which will not explode until workers are ready to use it.
Alfred Nobel   1867

Aha! I've just invented a fascinating toy! I fitted a cylinder with mirrors and bits of colored glass. When I turn it, it produces a kaleidoscope of patterns of colors.
Sir David Brewster   1816

On Your Own

Do you sometimes think of new inventions? Start a lab notebook. Jot down your ideas. Include notes on improvements you think of for other people's discoveries and inventions. Perhaps you will become a famous inventor!

Answers

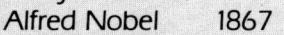

Toy Trivia

Discover the <u>who</u>, <u>when</u>, and <u>where</u> of these favorite toys of past and present.

It's nine o'clock. Mr. Thomas, owner of the toy shop, has gone home for the evening. He has pulled the shades and locked the door. But what is going on in the store? The toys have come to life! The robots are playing chess. The dolls are jumping rope. And the teddy bears are playing a game of toy trivia. Join them and test your toy trivia knowledge.

Read each numbered trivia card and choose your answers.

1. The first video game simulated a tennis match. This electronic game was called _____.

○ Pinball
△ Pac Man
□ Pong

2. To make classroom study more fun, a teacher from England, named John Spilsbury, cut up his lessons and invented _____.

○ Jigsaw puzzles
△ Flash cards
□ Bingo

3. In the 1940's the newest fad in Bridgeport, Connecticut was throwing pie tins. This was the forerunner to the toy known today as the _____.

○ Boomerang
△ Tambourine
□ Frisbee

4. The first talking doll was invented in Germany. What did the doll say?

○ "Hello"
△ "Mama"
□ "Mother"

5. Papa Christiansen first made these wooden toys during the early 1930's for his sons. What are these plastic building blocks called today?

○ Tinkertoys
△ Lego blocks
□ Lincoln Logs

6. Charles Darrow made a fortune pretending to make a fortune when he invented which game?

○ Life
△ Wheel of Fortune
□ Monopoly

7. In 1979 a Hungarian chess expert invented this six-sided brain teaser. What is it called?

○ Boggle
△ Mastermind
□ Rubik's Cube

8. In this word-building game, players make up crosswords on a gameboard with letter tiles. The game, patented in 1931, is called _____.

○ Parcheesi
△ Password
□ Scrabble

9. The electric train was invented by whom?

○ Joshua Lionel Cowan
△ Lionel Richie
□ Thomas Alva Edison

10. In 1958 this item started a craze that had the entire country swinging its hips. What was it called?

○ Hula skirt
△ Hula-Hoop
□ Yo-yo

Pong was the first of many video games that enjoyed success in the late 1970's and early 1980's.

John Spilsbury, a geography teacher, glued a map of England and Wales to a piece of wood. Using a saw with a "jigsaw" blade, he cut the map into pieces and had the children fit the pieces together again.

When he placed a small motor under the model of a railroad car, Joshua Lionel Cowan invented the model electric train. He used his middle name, Lionel, for the name of his toy train.

The real estate board game, Monopoly, was invented in 1933 by Charles Darrow. He sold his idea to Parker Brothers and turned his game into a real-life fortune for himself.

The German inventor, Johann Maelzel, created a device in 1824 that allowed dolls to say, "Mama." Maelzel is also known for his invention of the metronome for music.

Could you solve the puzzle of Rubik's Cube? The object of this brain teaser is to rearrange the squares so that each of the six sides is one solid color. The success of this cube earned its inventor, Erno Rubik, millions of dollars.

Scrabble, a word-building game, was invented in 1931 by Alfred M. Butts. The letter tiles with the highest point value are "Q" and "Z," with 10 points each.

The hottest craze of 1958 was the Hula-Hoop. Modeled after an Australian wooden toy, this plastic hoop provided hours of fun and exercise for both young and old.

The Frisbee Pie Company of Bridgeport, Connecticut was the probable supplier of pie tins to the town's children who spent hours tossing the tins to one another. In 1957 the WHAM-O Company began selling a plastic toy named the Frisbee.

The building toys known as Lego blocks were the brainchild of a Danish father. During the 1930's, Papa Christiansen made wooden toys to amuse his children. His son, Gotfried, later changed the wooden blocks to their present-day plastic and interlocking form.

On Your Own

Invent your own board game. Make the rules as wild and wacky as you wish. Use game pieces from old games you no longer use. Index cards make excellent playing cards.

Answers